THE GLIDE

Confessions of a Florida Surfer

Hunter Camp

The sea, once it casts its spell, holds one in its net of wonder forever.

Jacques Cousteau

Life is a succession of lessons which must be lived to be understood.

Hellen Keller

PREFACE

It's warm and breezy on the beach. The white sand is speckled with broken bits of shells and the heat of the sand feels good on my feet. The wind is balmy. The sun is hidden behind a late afternoon cloud, and I scan the ocean for any sign of a wave. The small surf is windblown and less than appealing. I watch and debate whether to paddle out.

Florida is known for its beaches, theme parks, oranges, over development, sunshine, and retirement communities. It's known for alligators, spring break, and the Everglades. But Florida isn't known for its waves, and for good reason: we rarely get great waves, at least compared to iconic places like California and Hawaii. But lack of good, consistent surf hasn't kept me, or thousands like me from chartering our lives by swells that are often less than desirable. Lack of good surf hasn't kept Florida surfers from organizing their days around the possibility of waves.

Life, like Florida surf, is a mixed bag. We go about our days piecing together what we imagine to be a good existence. We strive to live as we dream but we often don't take much time to reflect on the stuff of life, how we're living, or where our lives are taking us.

I mean, when was the last time that you really wondered about the parts and pieces of your life? When was the last time that you wondered about the thoughts, actions, accomplishments, failures, loves, and dreams that have shaped, and are shaping you into the person you may wish, or not wish to become? We all have journeys, and our lives are the sum of our experiences, DNA, relationships, passions, hopes, and plans. We are who we are because of factors both beyond our control and within our control. We are who we are because of choices we've made or situations that have been forced on us. Somewhere in the mix of all this, the divine figures in, however you might imagine the divine—if you imagine the divine.

My life has been a fusion of earthy elements like surfing, travel, pain, drugs, and love. My life has also been steeped in spirituality, even when I didn't believe in God. In every step along the way, I've been given to asking questions and seeking answers. Throughout it all, surfing has been a golden thread linking events and musings into the fabric of my consciousness.

As I stand on the beach and debate whether to surf the small, windblown waves, and as the sun warms my back, I decide, like 1,000 times before, today, that it only takes one fun wave to make my day.

I think I'll paddle out.

Hunter Camp

St. Augustine Beach, FL, 2022

Table of Contents

Figure: The author gliding on a tiny peeler.

1: Your Life

The Mexican soldier in a navy uniform with gold piping was pointing a machine gun at my chest. He didn't want to talk about surfing. The young man, with dark hair and pimples, didn't want to talk about the meaning of life or how the glide — surfing – is infused with spirituality. Although baby-faced, the soldier did his best to look tough, while seven of his friends stood nearby, smoking unfiltered cigarettes, laughing and smiling with crooked, butter-colored teeth. They watched my friend and me, believing we were drug runners. While the blazing sun melted the pavement and the waves sounded in the distance, they tore our truck apart looking for something we didn't have.

If you've never had an automatic rifle pointed at you, in earnest or otherwise, it's scary. It made me jittery. The long, black barrel with a small, eye-like hole can make you think about life. Your life. The purpose of it all.

It can make you think about where your life is headed and where you want it to go — and not go.

As the search of our truck progressed, I tried to make small talk about the rifle the young man aimed at me. Because I grew up with guns, I tried to win him over with my appreciation for the weapon. My olive branch fell flat. So, I offered to walk a couple of hundred feet to a taco stand. There, next to a gray shack and a large tree, an old woman in a white cotton dress rolled fried fish with fresh goat cheese in tortillas for fifty cents. The dust was thick in the air. Surely it was no coincidence that the soldiers had set up their roadblock next to a gritty place offering lunch and orange Fanta.

As I ordered lunch, I wondered why I was here, thousands of miles from my home in Florida where, while great surf was often lacking, there was a shortage of police pointing automatic rifles at me. I marveled at how surfing, and a love of adventure, had taken a suburban boy like me who grew up in a country club atmosphere to places Sunday School teachers warned their students about, if not directly then by insulation. Surfing – the glide – was, I knew, partly responsible for leading me, both physically and psychologically, into beautiful and questionable places and situations, some of which I confess in the pages that follow. At its root, the spirituality of the glide seduced me, and never let me go.

2: Florida Air

More than 25 years after the incident with the Mexican soldier, the glide remains spiritual to me. Today, the scorching summer sun hangs yellow and low on the horizon, soft and diluted in the morning haze, as if it were a dripping scoop of mango ice cream on an invisible cone. It's early and there's nothing yet fierce about the August heat. I didn't even bother with sunscreen — despite recently being cut on by my dermatologist. I know, I know. Not smart. Even if I had on full body armor and SPF 1000, my dermatologist would still scold me.

I look east, directly at the rising orb and wonder about life, its circuitous meaning, marveling at the unlikeliness of me becoming pastor of the oldest Presbyterian Church in Florida in the oldest city in the United States. Looking just above the rising sun, I see the sky, like the sun, is a soft pastel color. Combined, the sun and sky have the makings of an impressionist painting. The sky is an exceptionally light blue – a Tiffany blue – and without much depth, streaked with a film of white clouds stretching from north to south.

The Florida air, of course, is sticky, the humidity already high. But humidity doesn't bother me. Never has. It's like a familiar blanket. Many people mind the humidity, especially transplants from northern climates. During the full heat of summer, which can drive the heat index to 110, complaints about the humidity are incessant. I suspect, however, the complainers grumbled about the weather in whatever state they used to live in. When I hear people complain about the heat, I think of my Florida grandparents, their grandparents, and their grandparents who grew up without air conditioning or any modern convenience that has made Florida too accessible.

3: Waiting

I was born and raised in Florida, so named by the Spanish for its many flowers. But it's not easy to find many wildflowers on the coast these days. Condos, hotels, and homes have sprouted in what once were dunes and hammocks. I have watched Florida disappear, or transform, from a sub-tropical paradise to one long coastal strip mall. A surfing friend named Joe postulates that developments take their names from the habitats that they destroy. For example, you have places like Oak Haven, Palm Dunes, Marsh Place, and the like. He makes a good argument.

I've lived in Georgia, South Carolina, North Carolina, Virginia, and Colorado. I have traveled widely in the U.S. and abroad. I have surfed in multiple places inside and outside the continental U.S. But I always come back home to the northeast coast of the Sunshine State. I prefer the weather, the comfortable water temperatures, and the now fading Southern lifestyle that once dominated North Florida, including my ancestral home, St. Augustine, where I currently live and surf.

The ocean on this August morning is 83 degrees. My tanned legs dangle in the water as I straddle my longboard. The water has good clarity, a light green color that reminds me of the bayside of the Keys. It would be impossible for me to estimate how many times I have sat like this: posterior in baggies, sitting quietly and expectantly upon a waxed board in warm water, waiting for a wave. A surf monk in the cathedral of the olive-colored sea. This is my thirty-seventh-year surfing. It boggles my mind to attempt a wave count. It's like a golfer after thirty-seven years of golfing attempting to number how many times, she has smacked that little white ball. And if those who practice, enjoy, and dedicate themselves to hitting the little white ball are golfers, then when it comes to gliding upon waves, I am a surfer.

But I think of none of this as I sit on my 9-foot, 4-inch yellow, single-fin board waiting for a wave. A long time ago I recall seeing an advertisement in a surfing magazine that read: "Some people spend their lives waiting for nothing at all. I think I'll spend mine waiting for waves." There is something deep and important about the act of waiting for a wave. While not an end in and of itself, waiting for a wave is crucial to the glide. One is still, focused, maybe chatting with a friend, both of you staring at the ocean's horizon. While surfing is not meditation, it can be meditative. And while surfing is not prayer, it can be prayerful. The rhythms of the sea lull the one waiting for a wave into a deeper flow of consciousness. Breathe. Look. Breathe. Look. Stay in the present. In the moment. Don't think about a future that doesn't exist but stay present in the present. This act is deeply spiritual and very counter-cultural.

Sitting on my board staying present in the moment, I notice the way the morning light refracts off the ocean's surface. I notice the pelicans as they fly like gentle brown bombers over the surface of the water. I notice the shadows that these same pelicans cast upon a wave. I notice the sleek backs

6

of dolphins when they roll and blow air. I notice bait fish jumping out of the water trying to avoid some larger fish that's chasing them. I notice the feeling of the air in my lungs and the sun on my body. I notice how I feel in the moment, and which body parts ache or don't ache. I notice the sky and if there are clouds and what type of clouds. I notice the colors of the horizon and any sail or shrimp boats that dot the sea.

To stay in the present moment is to open oneself up to the fullest meaning of life, which can only be found in the present — because life exists

only in the present. The past and future are abstract ideas. They are not, as far as we know, alive, unlike the present.

4: Future

It's easy to slip into living for a future that may — or may not — ever arrive. It's also easy to slip into worrying about a past that no longer exists. It's easy to fall out of the present moment and into a hypothetical life. The Buddha said, "Do not dwell in the past, do not dream of the future, concentrate the mind on the present moment." Easier said than done. If you're like me, you might have a challenging time staying in the present moment. Even in the best of circumstances, my mind can race away, getting stuck in times that do not exist, except in the mind of God.

I remember one time when my family and I were vacationing in the Keys. Not a worry in the world. Totally relaxed. I was living the advice of philosopher Ralph Waldo Emerson: "With the past, I have nothing to do; nor with the future. I live now."

One afternoon while I was there, I was drinking a margarita in a tall, cold glass that dripped icy condensation, watching palm trees with green fronds blow in the breeze. Then, from out of nowhere, a thought popped into my head: "How long until we need to buy a new car? How long will the current car last? Will we have enough money when the time comes?"

Suddenly, my icy beverage no longer tasted so good. The palm trees lost their luster. Relaxation crumbled like a house of cards, all because I could not stay in the moment. All because my mind went racing to a future that may — or may not — ever exist. If only I could have been more like Jesus as I basked in the sun: "Do not worry about your life," said Jesus, "what you will eat, or about your body, what you will wear. For life is more than food, and body more than clothing."

There is a difference between being prepared for a future that does not yet exist (and may never exist) and being consumed by this not-yet existing future. We must plan. We must plot and save and try our best to predict. But living in a future that does not yet exist is futile. It is a killjoy. It is illusory. It is a self-made prison.

But at this moment, I am fully focused upon waiting for a wave. Depending on the swell and its size, if it is long-period or short-period, the act of waiting can take on different dimensions. A long-period swell is, at least for most surfers, the most desirable type of swell. When a swell is long-period, it comes from a greater distance. The winds have had a greater expanse of water to blow over (what meteorologists call fetch or fetch length). This greater fetch gives the energy in the water time to organize itself into sets of waves, and like good soldiers, march in a timely manner to your beach.

When we wait for waves, all senses are tuned into the horizon, to the least little bump that rises in the distance. When waves are spotted, a strong, silent hope fills the mind. The wait is over, if only for a moment. Surfers are people who spend hours upon hours doing nothing but waiting. We sit upon our boards like equestrians sit upon a horse — western-style. The waiting for waves is entirely non-productive. One does nothing but watch and wait. This waiting might appear to an outsider boring or listless. And sometimes it can become that. But, as a rule, waiting for a wave is full of anticipation—and anticipation is rarely boring.

It strikes me how poorly we Americans are at waiting — for anything. We live drive-thru lives. If we are not moving, we think we are wasting time, a commodity we can never acquire enough of. And yet, this constant momentum makes for a fractured life. We become frenetic beings, jerking here and there through the grocery store, at work, sitting at traffic lights, and fidgeting with our phones. We always wait, with some amount of impatience, for the next thing to happen. Many of us fear that we must always be doing something. Otherwise, we may appear useless or valueless, which makes for a meaningless life. We have been fooled into believing that busyness equates to worth. Surfing helps adjust this discontented attitude.

Generally, waiting for a wave is a peace-filled activity. I watch the horizon and the slow bob of the current rocks me back and forth. Sometimes I feel like a baby in a crib. Even on days with the biggest waves – which admittedly are not very large, adrenaline ebbs and flows with peace. I watch pelicans fly six inches above the surface of the water. Ospreys dive like twisted angels with talons. Manta rays breach the water, drops of water sliding from their backs like molten silver slipping from the hand of God. In moments like these, I've noticed that deep questions arise, questions like, "Who am I and who am I becoming?" I don't force these questions. They come of their own accord, like they are partners with the glide, helping me to become who God has meant me to be.

5: Barbados

As I sit on my board and wait, I look down into the water and I see my toes. I think of the marvel of the human body, our very skeletons fully recreated every 10 years, broken bones able to mend in eight weeks, a new layer of the epidermis, outer skin, every three wee weeks or so. The human body is a work of art. As I look at my toes dangling in the water, I wait.

Waiting is not always peaceful. Like in 1989 when I surfed a place called Duppies in Barbados. We arrived early in the morning, having driven from the northern tip of the island over dirt roads with crater size potholes. Lanky coco palms mimicked the lanky, dark women with children on their hips.

We sped through the countryside, a few battered work trucks on the road, passing young children with wide smiles waving as they walked to school. The island was very green. We drove the last one hundred yards down a bumpy dirt path stopping at the edge of a cliff. We piled out of the white van, which was stacked with nine surfboards. Six white Americans and one black Bajan guide-surfer. We looked at the waves and not a soul sat in the lineup. The corduroy lines were stacked as far as we could see. "Big waves, mon," said our guide.

From the top of the cliff to the water was, if memory serves, about two hundred feet. The waves broke about one hundred yards from the small cove at the bottom of the cliff. From the top of the cliff, the waves didn't look big. As a nineteen-year-old Florida kid, I did not yet know how height distorts wave size. To me, the waves simply looked like six feet of perfection peeling right into a wide channel. We walked the trail to the beach. At the bottom of the trail there was a dark cave, about twenty feet across. The waves shook the ground. Or, at least, I felt a tremor, which may have been my heart skipping beats. The waves were big. They sounded like dynamite. I felt queasy. We watched these perfect, very large waves for a few minutes and then decided to investigate the cave. I remember asking our guide, "Why are there bones everywhere?" He replied, "Voodoo, mon. Chicken bones from the witch doctor. He come here." I suddenly felt worse. A bad omen, I thought. I walked back up the cliff to contemplate whether I would paddle out.

Eventually, our guide and one member of our crew paddled out. The waves looked as tall as a telephone poll. I watched a member of our crew wipeout and lose his board, his leash snapping. He surfaced, swam in, and got a new leash. I followed him back out.

The channel was safe, and I paddled to the shoulder of the peak. I waited, sitting on my mini gun, which is a board designed to be ridden on larger waves. My heart pounded and my body was tight. This kind of waiting, waiting for a wave that has the potential to inflict serious bodily injury is fear-filled. Buzzy Trent, a famous surfer, once said, "Big waves are not measured in feet, but in increments of fear." I was scared. The waiting was not peace-filled and meditative but full of heightened awareness, senses tuned to a sharp edge, anxiety everywhere in my mind.

But today, as I wait in in the semi-transparent water off St.

Augustine Beach, it is all peace. I feel like a quiet monk, still and patient, full of acceptance and non-attachment. The waves are small, only a couple of feet—knee to waist high. The ocean is like a sheet of glass: oily slick and looking to the horizon, it appears opaque, even though I know that the farther out, the clearer the water becomes. The dark oily surface stretches into infinity, or at least all the way to Morocco, which is 4,291 miles due east from where I sit and along the same latitude and longitude. And there is not a soul out in the warm water. Except for one tarpon a dozen feet away, measuring about six feet long. The large tarpon rolls and eventually comes all the way out of the water, spooking me with its crash-landing as it chases some unlucky prey. Waiting alone for waves, even small waves is vastly different from waiting for waves with a friend, which itself is different from waiting for waves with another surfer you don't know but simply acknowledge.

6: Localism

Scenarios of surfing with people I don't know happens a lot at my home break. The St. Augustine area gets six million visitors per year. While most of these people visit the historic sites of the nation's oldest city, more than a few dots the beach and populate the surf. 30 years ago, localism was strong, but not so much anymore. There are so many people surfing here in St. Augustine that it's become hard to know who lives here and who does not.

Localism, as practiced in some places, is contrary to the spiritual nature of the glide. The glide should change those who practice it. The glide should open the heart rather than close it. It should humble the heart rather than inject it with pride or vanity, warm the heart rather than turn it cold.

I admit, however, that on good days when the water is rife with surfers, I can become more territorial and feel that I have an inalienable right to the waves that are breaking at "my spot," the one that I surf day in and day out, good or bad. I can become a little more aggressive in my stares, paddling, and calling people off a wave. Sometimes, though rarely, I have gone as far as to snake people, dropping in on them as they take a wave.

When the lineup has a lot of people, I will also paddle around them for the best position, but this is only good strategy. Having said this, the older I become the more I want to share waves. The more I want to offer waves to surfers I'm in the lineup with. The glide is slowly teaching me to be more generous, patient, and tolerant.

7: God

As I wait alone in waist-high waves. floating like a cork, I think about God. Not the boxed-in God that occupies most imaginations, whether religious or non-religious. Not a God with certain constraints imposed by the believer or nonbeliever. But a God that (or who?) can be whatever God wants to be to whomever God condescends. The God I consider while waiting alone for a wave is, as the existentialist philosopher and Protestant theologian Paul Tillich said, "The God above God."

God above God is the source of all our ruminations and abstractions about God.

The God above God cannot be defined with certainty or affirmed beyond saying the word "God," which is an English translation of a medieval German word, Gott. The God above God may be personal or impersonal, though I happen to believe that this God is personal, transcendent, and immanent. This wildly untamed force of being is incalculable — beyond philosophy, theology, piety, and science.

And while some religious traditions – including at times my own Christian tradition – may affirm that this God cannot be known outside their own religious tradition, I fully disagree.

I have intuited God while staring at the beauty and complexity of a spider web. Wet with dew, the sun makes the web sparkle with the mystery of a small universe. God's presence, to those who see, is discernable in every aspect of life — but it is particularly noticeable in the ocean.

8: A Wave

A wave rolls toward me, the energy beneath the water's surface pushing it along. It is sleek and soft, making its slow approach to my position. Many people have the wrong impression that a wave, in its singularity, has moved across the open expanse of the ocean, never changing in its waviness, that a singular wave has traveled as itself — a wave form — from a distant location to arrive at the beach. But this isn't true.

A wave is only a wave due to the energy beneath the water that travels from some distance to arrive at the beach. The bump on the horizon is a symbol of unspent energy pulsing outward. As the energy travels, it pushes water up and out (think of a bulldozer pushing sand up and out), causing what appears to be a singular phenomenon: an ocean wave. It is a reality in and of itself — a unit of energy. Until the last hiccup of its energy is spent, there is no singular wave upon the water. The wave you see on the horizon is the result of the energy beneath the surface of the water and, in essence, one long continuous chain of "waves." So, a wave is waves of subsurface energy. Surfers ride energy. We glide on the physical manifestation of an invisible force imagined and set in motion by God.

18

9: Paddling

As I paddle in a prone position to meet the oncoming energy that I will ride, I can't help but wonder at the God behind this unseen energy. I wonder if this God is pleased at those of us who glide. I wonder if this God surfs the cosmic energy of some distant exploding star or the energy of a black hole swallowing dark matter. Paddling to catch the small glassy wave, I use my deltoids, triceps, lats, and core. I feel the muscles moving on their own, trained over decades. I feel the muscles tightening and retracting as they should, pulling me into position on the feathering peak, the apex of the energy. I quickly spin, consciously slow my breathing, point my board, stroke twice and feel the pull, the seduction of sliding down the face of the wave. I jump to my feet, trying to step lightly. I now have the wave, or it has me, and for the next few seconds I think of nothing except the glide. Sometimes, in my better moments, I don't even think about the glide, but only feel and sense it.

Speeding down the line on the wave, my board pointing north, I see sunlight penetrating the curl as it bends to break. I make it to the shoulder, cut back to meet the curl, stall, go high and begin walking to the nose, then back-peddle, finishing the ride by jumping off and over the wave as my board is taken from beneath my feet and pulled toward the beach, washing onto the coquina sand with a scraping sound, the 9-inch fin digging in like an anchor.

A little girl, no more than five years old, with platinum blonde hair and a red bathing suit is collecting shells — mostly arcs — near my board. As I exit the water to retrieve my board she stops, looks, smiles, and points to the big yellow shape lying in the white sand. Her mother walks over, crouches in a blue bikini, and along with her daughter, watch as I pick the board up and turn to paddle back out. I can't help but wonder if I am the first surfer the little girl has ever seen. I wonder if seeing a surfer will inspire her to one day experience the glide herself.

The first time I saw a surfer was in the mid-to-late seventies. It was at Crescent Beach, which is about five miles south of where I now live. My family was gathered on the beach for a picnic. I recall only watching a guy surf one wave on an army green surfboard. But 44 years later, I still remember the day. Surfing spoke to me.

Maybe surfing will speak to the little girl in the red bathing suit. Things either speak to us or they do not. And sometimes something that did not speak to us as child will speak to us later in life. And sometimes something that spoke to us as a child will no longer speak to us as we age. I have played about every sport known to the western world. But only two activities have stuck with me since adolescence: surfing and fishing. Both are water-based and natural in their elements. Surfing is unlike tennis, which I dearly loved — loved enough to play on a high school team. Surfing is different from golf, which, again, I played with a passion on the high school team. While golf is played outside among trees and birds, – and in Florida, alligators – it is not a nature sport in the sense of uncultivated nature. Golf is a groomed sport, tamed and controlled nature, with commercial sand, all of which sits in the haze of necessary pesticides and herbicides to maintain the illusion of reality.

Not so in surfing. While it's true that some surf spots have a noxious amount of pollution and some waves are found in cement pools or created by wave-generating machines, as a rule, surfing is practiced in the wild of the ocean, amidst relatively clean water. The ocean is not just untamed, but untamable. We might manage the ocean, with jetties or bulkheads, for example, but the ocean is uncontrollable by humans.

While one might play the sport of golf on a given course a dozen times and while the course may play differently depending on the weather, it remains mostly the same. And, outside of lightning in the summertime and the occasional alligator found on the odd Florida hole, golf is safe. There is no overt risk. But surfing is never the same. Even where the wave is predictable based on the formation of the reef, the wave can change from day to day depending on the size and direction of the swell. No wave is like the wave that precedes it. Each wave is distinct unto itself.

As I paddle back out through the calm emerald colored water, I glance to the beach and see the little blonde girl and her mother, both hunched over like migrants digging up potatoes. They search for the perfect shell as I look to the horizon for the perfect wave — even among waist-high glass there is a perfect wave. Each session has its own perfect wave, which is another way to the say the wave of the day. And always, the wave of the day is the wave where the greatest fun abounds, where play is lifted to a holy pursuit

10: Looking for Waves

Looking for waves is a good metaphor for life. In some sense and to some degree, we all make our way through life looking for that perfect wave, r, at least, we are always searching for something to add beauty to our lives. We hunt and peck scouring and surveying life in the hope of finding that one thing that will remove us from the ordinary to some lofty place where our deepest hunger calls out. We look to things – to family, new surfboards, waves, cars, clothes, lovers, phones, friends, social media, money, food, work, music, art, rum, animals, and to our children – in hope of finding an emotional pacifier. We are like children hunting for that special shell to remind ourselves of some fantasy-life we have created in our minds.

11: Perfection

I wait, again, for a wave. The waiting never ends. It never gets tedious because every surfer carries hope in his or her chest, to paraphrase Emily Dickinson. We are ever hopeful sitting on our boards, long or short. Hoping for that perfect wave, which is an illusion of sorts, like every other construct of perfection. Nevertheless, we continue to be hope-filled people, casting our silent prayers to the horizon.

Perfection does not exist, except in the mind of God, cults, and Platonic philosophy. That being said, one might argue that every wave is perfect, in so far as it is what it is: every wave is exactly what it was generated to become. Each wave is exactly what the physics of its energy, contours of the bottom, swell direction, and wind determine it to be. It, the wave, is itself. We would do well to emulate the nature of a wave. Perfection, if it does exist in any form outside the abstract, exists solely in the eye of the one observing a wave, piece of art, a flower, or a person. Perfection is a state of mind, not a realized form of being.

But that doesn't keep me, or any other surfer from looking for the wave that makes us feel the holy tremor of an exquisite glide. Those moments of excellence have come to me while surfing a peeling glassy 1-foot wave on a sandbar to a double-overhead reef break. The feeling of the glide determines our feelings for the wave. If the feeling of a particular glide reaches our standard of perfection, then the wave is considered to be perfect. Again, a wave is, in and of itself, always perfect. It is our experience of the wave that determines our perception of its perfection. Truth be told, the holy tremor of an exquisite glide does not strike me in waves where fear becomes a major factor in play. For some surfers, of course, the fear is exactly where the holy tremor of an exquisite glide begins. But not me. I like a good head-high day with light offshore winds and 80-degree water. Nothing too big but big enough to thrill me with a little speed and a barrel (getting inside the wave), which is the moment, bar none, that serves as the litmus test for the purest form of ecstasy.

In my life, there have only been two other experiences that have exceeded the joy of being tucked inside the sea with the sound of the churning water behind me, nothing visible to the right or left only light straight ahead. I imagine it is the closest sensation possible to being in our mothers' wombs.

12: Pure Light

When I was 26 years old, I entered Mepkin Abbey, a Trappist monastery outside of Charleston, SC. It was started by the Abbey of Gethsemane in Kentucky, which was the home monastery of one of the great 20th century mystics, Thomas Merton, who is known the world over for his books and wisdom, which encompassed and expanded to include not only his native Christian tradition but also his appreciation of Zen Buddhism. While I was in the monastery, I had an experience that left me, and continues to leave me, speechless. It was an experience that carried me, as St. Paul might say, into the seventh heaven. The joy was so intense that for three days I could not stop weeping. It altered the way I understand life and exposed the very thin veil that separates us from a greater reality — God.

It happened like this: In the afternoon I met with the Abbot, the father of the monastery. He was a plain-looking, middle-aged man. He had short, neatly trimmed black hair and large, thick glasses. His face had pock marks from acne. He was not a pretty man nor did his appearance inspire the imagination. He was plain and a bit aloof. He was the youngest Abbot this monastery had ever seen.

I was made to wait a couple of minutes on a couch outside his study. He invited me in. His study was not ornate or exotic, but it wasn't commonplace, either. He had shelves full of books and a computer. The study could have been that of a parish pastor or professor.

After we talked for a few minutes about my life and life at the abbey, he then began to talk about the importance of meditating on the love of God — how much God loves the world and each person in the world. As the Abbot spoke, I began to sense something odd, which is difficult to describe. It was as if a warm light, soft and brilliant, penetrated my mind and body. I saw light behind my eyes, in front of my eyes, all around the room, thin sheets of it, sharp and bright but not sharp and burning. It felt good, comforting, to see the light, even though the experience was confusing.

Then something else happened. I sat in the warm light enjoying the presence and the feeling of what I believe was God's Spirit. Suddenly, it was as if I was being lifted off my chair. I felt as if I was floating above my seat. I wondered silently to myself, "Does the Abbot notice that I'm floating?" I wondered to myself if the Abbot noticed how the room was being changed into pure light. Floating above my chair, I kept waiting for the Abbot to say something that would recognize my situation. But he didn't, of course, because he didn't experience me the same way I experienced me.

I wondered to myself, "What's happening to me?" Then the light and the sense of floating disappeared as quickly as it emerged.

The second greatest joy in my life that is equivalent to, or even supplants a fine and perfect barrel, was the birth of my only child. Like my experience in the monastery, it was a mystical experience of the highest order.

Nothing could have prepared me for the extreme emotion that I felt when he crowned and finally wiggled out into the waiting arms of the midwife.

Today, however, on these thigh-high waves the sense of perfect joy comes to me, not in the glide itself – because the glides are short-lived – but in the waiting for the glides. The feeling of the sun warming my shoulders, turning them browner than a berry, beads of ocean water stuck on the flesh of my deltoids and forearms looking like raindrops. I look at the drops of water and I can almost see my reflection in them. And that is profound. To see oneself in a drop of the ocean.

I have always loved the sensation of the sun drying ocean water on my skin. My dark honey-colored pores tighten under the UV rays full of salt and heat. And while my dermatologist scolds me at each checkup, I always tell him that I enjoy the sun too much to stay out if it or even to wear long sleeve rash guards. I am a native Floridian. A child of the sun. This way of living may end up being the death of me through skin cancer, but I resolved some time ago to live the way I want to live, albeit with calculated risk. I do not want to die in the halls of a nursing home. I have seen too many people die in diapers, drooling, tubes feeding them. Not me. And yet, no matter how our life ends, I am certain that there is life beyond this life. I am certain that the light I experienced in the monastery waits for us all.

13: Regret

My maternal grandmother once lamented that our family, having arrived in St. Augustine in 1832 (for the second time, which was after the Spanish departed), did not purchase miles of beachfront property. "Such a missed opportunity, she said." All of us, I imagine, can relate to missed opportunities. All of us can relate to standing on the sidelines only to regret our inaction at a later point. Robert Fulton, an artist, and engineer was responsible in the early 1800's for putting sailing ships out of business. He made the steamboat a standard on the open seas. It is said that he presented his idea to Napoleon. After a few minutes of this presentation, Napoleon is reported to have said, "What, sir? You would make a ship sail against the wind and currents by lighting a bonfire under her decks? I pray you excuse me. I have no time to listen to such nonsense."

As a pastor, I am privy to stories of regret from people who missed adventure only to later bemoan the botched opportunity. Lost opportunities always have a common question at their core: "Why didn't I take the chance?" An Arabian proverb given to me by a Rotarian friend is true: "Four things do not come back: the spoken word, the sped arrow, the past life, and the neglected opportunity." All of us know that fumbled opportunities do not come back. Some of us live our lives lamenting a chance never taken. We look back upon something that we wish we would have done, but for fear we played it safe. We should all take advice from the Jewish Talmud, "Act while you can: while you have the chance, the means, and the strength."

My experience suggests that we often regret with great pathos those things that we did not do but wished we had done. For example, a common regret is not traveling when you have the health to travel. As the sun sets upon our lives, we have but memories. These memories are of two classes, either seized opportunities or regrets of inaction. I suppose it's often fear that keeps us from taking a chance. Fear of what might happen. Fear of the unknown. Fear of potential consequences. And, if we live too much by the dictates of fear, then we live on the periphery of life. Fear is antithetical to a life well-lived. As each year passes into the next, the more convinced I become that Mark Twain was correct when he wrote: "Twenty years from now you will be more disappointed by the things you didn't do than by the ones you did. So throw off the bowlines. Sail away from the safe harbor. Catch the trade winds in your sails. Explore. Dream. Discover."

I knew a good man who worked hard. He did not take many vacations. He saved. He planned for his early retirement. One year before he retired, he built his dream home in the mountains. A beautiful place with sweeping views of a valley forest and a strong river. He drew satisfaction from the future that he had created in his mind. He was going to fish, hike, and revel in the views. And so, he retired a man full of plans and ambitions. Six months into his early retirement he called me. The words came through the phone: "I've got stage 4 pancreatic cancer…" Six months later he was

29

dead. I could tell stories like this all day. It's nothing unusual. What is unusual is for someone to take this moment — this moment — seriously enough to understand that each second is important because there may not be another second.

Prior to marrying, my wife and I were the center of several parties. At one of these engagement parties, we sat in a large circle and each guest took a turn giving one or both of us advice. The last man in the circle, a psychiatrist, said in a flat and serious tone, "Contemplate your death daily. It will help you appreciate life." An early Christian monk once gave similar advice: "Those who keep death ever before them do not despair of life."

14: How We Glide

I wear sunscreen as a precaution, but I refuse to stay out of the sun or to cover my body with clothes to prevent what may or may not happen in a future that may or may not exist. I do not court death, but I refuse to kowtow to a fear inspired by a future that is not material. To a large degree, my mildly cavalier attitude toward death has come to me from two back-to-back health issues, which threatened my life, or at least the life that I had come to love and trust. Both situations involved surfing, one indirectly and one directly.

The first issue developed just after I turned forty years old. It was the second week of April. A Monday. After a surf session, I joked with my friend Joe about my left deltoid becoming overly buff. I suggested it must be all the pushups I was doing. Later that same day as I drove from my church to Starbucks, I began to touch my left deltoid, massaging the muscle. It was then that I noticed something odd: the thing I had mistaken as a growth in muscle was, in fact, a different kind of growth. It was the kind that moves under the skin when it is pushed or pulled. And the more I felt the area, the more I sensed that the thing in my deltoid was an identifiable mass — a separate entity, not part of the muscle structure.

My heart pounded as I stopped at a traffic light. I pulled off the road and called my primary physician, whom I saw that same day. He was not a good liar when said to me, "Hunter, I don't know what it is, but I want you to have an MRI done immediately." I know from experience that an MRI is not immediately ordered for no compelling cause, only a cause that has the potential to be dire.

The condensed version of this protracted story is that the orthopedic surgeon at the Mayo Clinic in Jacksonville said, "Hunter, it doesn't look good. The tumor is wrapped around and inside the humerus. You need to be prepared for radiation." Then she paused, looked at me and my wife, Amy, with some amount of sympathy and said, "You may lose your left arm. We won't know with any certainty until surgery."

Her words, "You may lose your left arm" sent small shock waves through my head. I felt queasy and lightheaded. The whole situation took on a surreal feeling. Amy looked over at me. I could see her internally steeling herself against what may become a vastly different life for us. Surgery was scheduled for the following week.

A week after surgery, the pathology report came back. We waited in one of the rooms until the doctor's physician's assistant, a thin man in his forties tapped on the door and walked in. After exchanging a few pleasantries, the PA said, "Well, we don't know what to say except, the Big Guy was watching out for you. The tumor, the size of a lemon, was benign." I had been given a new lease on life.

Even now, twelve years later, whenever I surf without a shirt, which is whenever the water is warm (about 8 months per year) I see the scar running vertically from the top of my left deltoid to the beginning of my bicep. Over time, the scar has shrunk from an ugly eight-inch-long reminder to a thin four-inch smooth patch of skin, barely visible. To help me never forget the grace that is mine, I have an eight-pointed star tattooed on the outside of my left deltoid. The eight-pointed star is a medieval Christian symbol of a new creation, a new beginning.

We are all, more less, new creations. Each day we are presented with a new wave to ride—and to some degree, we have the power to choose how we will ride our waves. We can choose to ride our waves with patience, gentleness, and kindness. Or we can choose to ride our waves like a jerk, scowling at people, dropping-in on people, or paddling like we own the sea – which we don't. Life is like surfing. Or surfing is like life. Either way, we have choices to make. How will we glide?

The concept of freewill is one of the thorniest theological conundrums. How much choice do we really have within the choices we make? Are our choices wholly, partly, or not at all determined by a higher power? How much freedom do we have within the specter of our lives? Do our current choices merely reflect our psychology or biology or some combination thereof? Are our current choices determined by our past choices? Are we products of our conditioning and thus not free to make an undetermined choice? Regardless of the answers to these questions, how we live matters. How we glide through life matters. Someone once said, "Surfing is life, the rest is detail." This is a sad and rather shallow perspective on the complexity and beauty of life. This slogan, while a great marketing byline once found in surfing magazines, is not fit for the heart of a surfer. How we live and surf matters. No matter how much or little freewill we possess, we are responsible for how we glide.

As I think about my personal responsibility for how I surf, I wait for a wave as the sun creeps higher into the long eastern sky. To my left is a young blonde surfer boy, probably 8 or 9 – a grom, as surfer kids are called. He has just paddled out. I see him, his dad, and older sister surfing on a regular basis. The boy's mother and younger sister take pictures from the beach.

Today, the boy is in the ocean by himself, but the rest of the clan are in various stages of dismounting from their bikes and are waxing boards. The dad is thin and all muscles, bald, and around my age, though age is always tough to tell with those who spend too much time in the sun. The dad rides a short board like the rest of his family. They all surf very well. The kids have sponsor's names on their boards. The oldest and youngest sister both have long, sandy blonde hair. The mother is lithe with long brown hair and is always present but never surfs. She stands on the beach with a long-lens camera. They remind me of a small tribe, a pack.

Today, the older daughter paddles out on a longboard, and I wait to see how she will ride. Aggressive or graceful? Nose or tail? Arms up or down or in T-posture? Her first wave says it all. She is like a cat. Light-footed. Her steps are full of poise. She is probably fourteen. She walks on the board like a dancer, and I am reminded of how often I am heavy-footed. I blame it on age. Her dad now wades into the small surf to watch his children. He doesn't have his board. After I catch a little right peeler and kick out next to where he is standing, I offer him my board to catch a couple of waves. He declines, saying, "It's fun to just watch the kids." I know that feeling. It's fun watching my son catch a wave. But I have some regrets. I wish I had not put him on a board when he was 3 years old. It scared him. He felt pressure from me to perform. I pushed him too hard to love surfing the way I love surfing. I didn't give him the freewill of choice.

No one should push another person to love anything that their heart does not know. Sometimes you can want something so badly for another person that you force its antithesis. This happens in sports, business, religion, and love. If you must force something on someone, the something you force is not a natural fit. And the result, as many parents know from experience, is a disdain or even hatred for a sport or business, religion, or relationship. Children also may come to hold a grudge against the tyrant who forced them to play at something that they did not love.

15: Happiness

I don't know who first made the remark, but my spouse is fond of saying to my son and me, "Do you want to be right or happy?" It's a good question, as the two may, at times, be mutually exclusive. For example, and to put the matter in domestic terms, would I rather argue with my wife to prove a point, or simply agree to disagree and maintain my own happiness (and her happiness, too, I might add)?

Psychological studies consistently demonstrate that we are consumed with the pursuit of happiness, to borrow a phrase from the Declaration of Independence. Even as far back as Aristotle, who wrote, "Happiness is the meaning and purpose of life," people have hunted for ways to make happiness a constant fixture in their lives. Typically, I'm not one to disagree with such a great mind, but I don't think Aristotle was correct. Happiness may have been his meaning and purpose in life, but it's not mine. I'm not denying that happiness is a strong motivating factor in my life, I simply disagree with Aristotle's conclusion.

Although an increasing number of people in our culture do regard happiness as the meaning and purpose in life, and while surfing may tend in this direction, I am inclined to agree with the historic religious traditions of the world. Those traditions teach that happiness is not an end in itself, but a by-product of a higher goal, and that happiness is best when shared. "Thousands of candles can be lit from a single candle," said the Buddha "and the life of the candle will not be shortened. Happiness never decreases by being shared." And from Hindu scripture, we read, "True happiness consists in making others happy."

As I go about my daily life, grocery shopping, pumping gas, or talking to random people at the farmer's market, it occurs to me that we may be losing a simple conviction that runs through the world's major religions. In the words of the Christian New Testament: "It is better to give than to receive." And why is it better? According to Gallup polls, people who share — people who seek to help other people — are happier people. My own experience suggests that this is true. My own happiness seems proportionally tied to my generosity and my willingness to extend a hand to others in need — or to share waves with strangers in the water, which is not an easy thing for a surfer at an established location.

Not long ago, Dr. Elizabeth Dunn at the University of British Columbia, Vancouver investigated the "giving equals happiness" equation. Dr. Dunn's research concluded that people are much happier if they spend money on gifts for others or on charitable donations— rather than spending it on themselves. It's my conviction that God formed us this way. We are created to know the greatest happiness when we extend ourselves for the sake of others. Of course, I may be wrong. But I'm not going to argue the point—because I prefer to be happy.

However, happiness is not the end-goal of life. Happiness, like hanging ten, is not always possible or always sustainable. Life, as well as surfing, is fluid. Happiness comes and goes. It's like the tide. Change is the only constant variable.

16: Soul Surfers

I s life like surfing or is surfing like life? I don't yet know, but I do know that the soul of surfing is an argument that has played out in surf magazines, surf shops, surf clubs, surf films, and social media.

I'd wager that most surfers agree that surfing has a soul — an immaterial part of the experience that undergirds the glide. It is a substance that can't be seen but only intuitively known. And it is this something that gives surfing its deep and resonant appeal that exceeds the physical act of riding a wave. The term, "Soul Surfer" stands in contrast to the person chasing the trophy, photo, or sponsor — be they longboarders or shortboarders. To use the glide to further some material benefit is not soul-surfing. Someone might argue that a surfer could use the glide to reap a material benefit so that more glides might be made. It's a valid argument. But it's not soul-surfing. To chase notoriety is not to chase the soul. The argument of "What is the soul of surfing?" is further developed and qualified by age, experience, and type of board. Who is the soul surfer? What makes someone a soul surfer? Do soul surfers have a more intimate connection to the glide, to the waves, to the heart of the art than the pro running after rankings on the World Cup Tour?

The dispute about the soul of surfing has been an undercurrent in the surfing community since the advent of the shortboard — at least. Part of me could care less about the argument over who is a soul-surfer and who is not a soul-surfer, as if the real or true soul-surfer is somehow verifiable by anyone. We may have opinions on who is a soul-surfer and who is not. But they are only that: opinions on a subject that means nothing to the world at large — and increasingly nothing to the surfing community.

There are, of course, some who would even deny that surfing has anything like a soul. These "soul deniers" suggest that surfing is only body mechanics and wave psychology. To the degree or extent that a surfer believes that surfing has a soul, a mysticism envelops the meaning of the glide. To me, surfing has a soul of sorts. And the longer I glide the more I feel that I am participating in something larger than myself — something immaterial that transcends ocean, wave, and glide. Surfing has become, for me, a mystical exercise of deep spiritual significance.

I had been surfing for years before I began to intuitively grasp that surfing is more than the simple (however complex) act of riding on the surface of water. I suppose I was about twenty years old when I had this realization. I was surfing my local break, FA, on St. Augustine Beach. It was fall and the air was crisp. The water was still warm. The western sky slowly began to turn the color of cotton candy as the sun sank into the horizon like a coin into a slot. The waves were good. Head high plus and glassy. A shower had just passed, and the water was smooth as oil. The wind was still. The heavens were turning soft shades of pink, orange, and blue with dashes of gentle white patches stirred around and through the prism of colors. Sitting in the lineup, waiting for a wave, the art of the glide began to slowly take on a different dimension. It was more than fun. It bordered on beatific. The water reflected the molten sky and I felt like Alice stepping through the looking glass. Things looked different. I sensed that I was interfacing with something much grander than mere happiness, much more ecstatic than play. Waiting for a wave and catching waves became an exercise in holiness. A sacredness enveloped the ocean and me within it. I recall the evening with great vividness and how I was transfixed by beauty of the highest order.

Beauty is a conduit of meaning. While I began to grasp the importance of beauty for the surfing life – for a life well-lived life in general – and how beauty inspires the surfer to live in the moment, it wasn't until I was forty-one that the power of beauty took on a deeper, more pressing significance.

17: Pain

In September 2010, while surfing a disorganized but Florida-style large swell from Hurricane Igor, I suffered a tremendous wipeout. The wipeout was a freakish event. I knew immediately that something was very wrong with my body. For the next year, I was close to being bed-ridden, and always in pain, unless I had drunk enough alcohol or taken enough painkillers, or was sound asleep. I did continue to serve my church parish — but the work was an exercise in growing frustration, depression, and despair. I could work, but that was essentially all I could do. When I was off, I would sit idly in a chair on our back deck or lie on a couch in our living room. I would do my best to remain statue-like. The more I moved the more I hurt. The pain in my core never ceased, except when I was asleep or strongly medicated.

I went from physician to physician seeking a diagnosis. I spiraled into despair. I began to contemplate suicide — not because I wanted to die but because I wanted the pain to end. Even the famed Mayo Clinic was, at first, no help. It was only after my third visit to Mayo that a diagnosis was suggested. "Athletic Pubalgia" said the head of the orthopedic department. I recall feeling elated that a diagnosis had been rendered, if only tentatively. I remember saying, "OK. When can you fix it?" And then the words, "We can't fix it. There are only two surgeons in the world that do this surgery with success. One is in Philadelphia and the other is in Germany." Two weeks later I was in Philadelphia. The surgery for my sports hernia was successful. But after nine months of doing extraordinarily little to nothing with my body, it took another six months to get back to where I could surf.

During the period between injury and recovery, I began to appreciate the power of beauty through the medium of art — specifically paintings hanging on our walls. Over the years, my wife and I have collected some by the Highwaymen, a group of mostly now dead Black men and one Black woman who lived in the Ft. Pierce, Florida, area. They painted the landscapes of coastal Florida from the Indian River west to the cattle country of the piney woodlands. The Highwaymen have a cult-like following among some people in Florida. The paintings are filled with vibrant colors depicting the ocean, lagoons, palm trees, sunsets, and moonlight. Prior to surgery, and as I spent my evenings lying on our couch, I would stare at these paintings and imagine myself inside their scenes. Two paintings inspired me.

One of the paintings was not actually a Highwayman — but a piece painted by their teacher, "Beanie" Backus. His work has been hailed as the finest ever produced in Florida native landscapes. The painting we own was done in 1948 and was given to me by my now deceased grandmother. Backus' work is alive. It comes off the canvas. The painting that hangs on our wall, is a simple scene: a coco palm in the foreground, green fronds stretched like a hand of fingers into the soft blue sky dotted with cumulus clouds. To the left of the palm is a mangrove and, in the background, the Indian River is visible. But this painting – its beauty – it gave me hope. In part, it gave me hope

43

because I could easily imagine myself reclining next to the palm, the breeze in my hair, the sun shining fiercely, the smell of the river that feeds into the ocean, and the sound of palm fronds scraping against one another. The feeling of being without pain. The feeling of being whole. Lying on the couch, still as death, I could smell the Atlantic and feel the sand beneath my feet.

Staring at this painting by Backus, I was transposed into life. Beauty has such power. Beauty can inspire hope. I believe that hope, despite what St. Paul said, is greater than faith or love. Without hope no amount of faith or love is going to rescue the person trapped in depression. In my life, God used hope as a life preserver.

18: Beauty

I f I were to argue about the soul of surfing, I would suggest that soul — a certain mystique and holiness — is present in surfing. But this mystique is not accessible to all people, primarily because they are not in tune with beauty. Appreciation of beauty — aesthetics — is more than being able to check out a good-looking person sunning on the beach. Appreciation of beauty takes work and practice. Attention and intention are required. A certain quietness of mind. And this quietness of mind is not easily had in our fractured, buzzing culture.

Sex appeal is often mislabeled as beauty, tricking boys and girls, men, and women into thinking that beauty is the same as physical affect. Sex appeal has its place. But sex appeal is different from beauty. Beauty comes from a deeper realm. It is transcendent. It is not necessarily sensual and may not be erotic. Beauty is healing. It is transformative. It inspires the beholder to greater awareness of the universe. Beauty is a portal by which the surfer touches deeper layers of the glide.

I am not an expert on beauty. I am not a professional aesthete. As an undergraduate at Flagler College, I was, however, a philosophy major where

I did study aesthetics. I even considered becoming a professor of philosophy. But God had other plans for me, at least professionally speaking. I went to graduate school, studied theology, and pursued a Master of Divinity (how silly is that title?) and followed the path to the vocation of Minister of Word and Sacrament, or Pastor in the Presbyterian Church (USA). So, while I may not be a professional philosopher who can talk about the rubrics and paradigms of beauty as described by great world thinkers and artists, I do know that part of the glide is beauty. When we glide, we dip our toe into the pond of God's very being, which must be beauty for who or what can create the wonders of the universe without being partly inspired by or moved by beauty? If God is anything comprehendible, God is beauty no less than God is love. When we appreciate or meditate upon beauty, to some micro-degree, we appreciate and meditate upon God.

When I'm sitting in the ocean waiting for a wave, as I stare at the endless horizon dotted with clouds or a simple expanse of blue, the beauty washes over me and I feel in tune with something far beyond myself, which I take to be God. And while some Christians will assert that God is only known through the person and work of Jesus, I agree with Martin Luther who stated that the Good News of God's love is found in the natural world. If we can only discover God through a singular source, Jesus, then what does that say about all that God has created. A rolling dolphin or a jumping manta ray inspires me to imagine God as much as reading any of the Gospels. It is the beauty of these animals that opens my mind to God's impact and aliveness.

Theology, at least historical theology, says nothing about the glide. History itself, up to the 1950's, says little about the glide. There is the one exception from the 1778 log of Captain Cook that describes the Hawaiian royalty riding waves. Cook wrote, "I could not help concluding this man had the most supreme pleasure while he was driven so fast and so smoothly by the sea." Cook visited the islands three times but on his third visit he was killed by natives. He never did get to surf.

The shelves of theology and its interpretation of surfing — a surfing theology or a theology of surfing — are not to be found. There have been some very engaging and important works related to surfing, such as *Caught Inside* by Daniel Duane and *Barbarian Days* by William Finnegan, which won a Pulitzer Prize. Be this as it may, I cannot help but think, as the sun bakes my face brown while I wait for another wave, that God gave us the glide because there are few pursuits in life more bliss-filled or beautiful than surfing. If there is a heaven in any literal sort of manner, it must be made, at least partially, with waves. Energy plus water equals heaven. That is my theology of surfing.

Even though there is a dearth of words written on a theology of surfing, this shouldn't keep us from musing about the One who is purported to have walked on water. Whether you believe or disbelieve the claims of Christianity, namely, that a guy named Jesus who lived 2,000 years ago is the very embodiment of God, this is irrelevant to the narrative integrity of the gospel story where Jesus walks on water. There is a difference between historical fact and spiritual truth. Spiritual truth does not need historical facts to exist or to offer a compelling vision. Narrative truth, spiritual truth, transcends historical fact.

In the story of Jesus walking on the water, which is found is three of the four canonical gospels, we see something like to the glide. In Matthew chapter 14, we read:

22 Immediately He made the disciples get into the boat and go ahead of Him to the other side, while He sent the crowds away. 23 After He had sent the crowds away, He went up on the mountain by Himself to pray; and when it was evening, He was there alone. 24 But the boat was already a long distance from the land, battered by the waves; for the wind was contrary. 25 And in the fourth watch of the night He came to them, walking on the sea. 26 When the disciples saw Him walking on the sea, they were terrified, and said, "It is a ghost!" And they cried out in fear. 27 But immediately Jesus spoke to them, saying, "Take courage, it is I; do not be afraid."

And then Peter, one of his disciples, asks Jesus to allow him to walk on walk. Peter wants to experience the glide. The story continues:

28 Peter said to Him, "Lord, if it is You, command me to come to You on the water." 29 And He said, "Come!" And Peter got out of the boat, walked on the water, and came toward Jesus. 30 But seeing the wind, he became frightened, and beginning to sink, he cried out, "Lord, save me!" 31 Immediately Jesus stretched out His hand and took hold of him, and said to him, "You of little faith, why did you doubt?" 32 When they got into the boat, the wind stopped. 33 And those who were in the boat worshiped Him, saying, "You are certainly God's Son!"

In biblical tradition, both Jewish and Christian (and other cultures, as well), water represents chaos. It was something beyond control and full of mystery. It had power. It was alive, moving with the wind, which was also alive with power. But here is a guy, a Palestinian Jew under the Roman

48

occupation, who treads on chaos, tramples fear, and conquers mystery with a power greater than anything they had ever known.

Mystery is a thread that is ever part of surfing. The glide has seduced many young surfers partly due to its mystery, which is a spirit of adventure. Why does it feel so good to move upon the surface of the ocean? What is it about the glide that makes a surfer want more of the same—pushes the surfer to explore far and wide, dare storms and senseless dangers, chance getting fired from jobs? It is, at least partly, the substance of mystery. And this mystery is close to the mystery of religious sensibilities. This mystery is like what prompted St. Peter to dare say, "Lord, if it is You, command me to come to You on the water." And He said, "Come!" And Peter got out of the boat, walked on the water, and came toward Jesus." To walk on the water is Godly and it is mysterious. Surfing is as close to walking on water as most of ever get.

19: Mystery

I remember a swell that I decided to surf in Anastasia State Park, which is near my home. I pedaled my bike, longboard slung on the side of the bike, to Blow Hole, a classic if now rarely surfed spot in the state park. It was early in the late spring. The fog was thick — San Francisco thick. The buoys were showing a good swell — 4 feet at 10 seconds from the east-northeast. It was offshore and I pedaled through the fog, tires munching sand and shell as I headed north. Fog wet my beard. Waves sounded beyond what I could see. The ocean was invisible. I could hear the surf breaking on the outside sandbar. There was only the sound of the surf, the sand beneath my tires, and my labored breathing from pedaling my bike. I could see about ten feet. The feeling of mystery, adventure, and beauty hung in the damp air.

Paddling out, I didn't know what to expect. When would I need to turtle my board or dive off? So, I paddled into mystery, the unknown, the secretive promise of beauty and fun. Although I don't know how, I timed the sets perfectly, and made it to the outside without even getting my hair wet. The waves were shoulder-to-head high coursing through at regular intervals. But still, alone in the fog and the mystery, I could see nothing beyond ten feet. The only wave I recall was the first, and I sped down the slick line with a wicked smile on my face, enjoying the speed.

Maybe that's how Jesus felt as he glided across the Sea of Galilee calling out to his disciples. Maybe Jesus was stoked to stand upon the watery chaos, feeling the energy of the water touch his toes and soles of his feet.

It's been my experience that at times when I'm thick into mystery, I often entertain the deepest of questions, like "Who am I?" Sitting alone in the ocean surrounded by fog, I remember wondering where God was leading me in life and who I was becoming as I approached middle age. Just because one gets older doesn't mean that change in life is dead. God is alive and life is fluid, exactly like the ocean. Mystery and adventure, combined with beauty, are agents of immense possibility.

20: Stoke

The stoke is the sum of the mystery. Matt Warshaw in his *Encyclopedia of Surfing*, writes that stoke is slang for "excited, pleased, happy, thrilled." It is certainly these things — but stoke is more than such things. Stoke runs deeper than mere happiness. Stoke brings contentment and joy, a sense of meaning and fulfillment. Stoke brings a childlike wonder to life. Stoke is surfing slang but it is also, in some respects, a philosophical term that is the very underpinning of all life. Without stoke there would be no life. Like life itself, stoke can be a noun or a verb, as in "The stoke from surfing is why I continue to surf, or "I'm stoked that I got to surf today."

The etymology of the word stoke is contested. But I imagine the word coming into existence around a campfire on some isolated beach. After a sweet day of riding waves, the surfers gather around a fire to cook some fish and drink some beer. The fire has been stoked by someone and it burns brightly making the surfers feel warm and cozy, mellow and happy. They share a sense of contentment about their day, which has been full of life. And then one of the surfers says to no one in particular, "Man, I'm stoked like this fire." And then a reply comes, "Stoked. Good word for this day, for surfing." And the rest is legend and myth.

21: Surf Trips

My first surf trip was when I was 16 years old. It was the summer of my junior year of high school, which also happened to be the year my parents divorced. My mother took my brother and me to California. We drove a little red car from San Francisco to Los Angeles on the Pacific Coast Highway. We stayed in small motels as we traced the coast.

To a boy born and raised in Florida, California was like a different world. The green rounded mountains near Carmel that came to the edge of the sea were unlike anything I had ever seen. Just north of Carmel, I saw a cut on the side of the cliffs that led down to the ocean. It was morning. The air was damp and cold. I pulled on my wetsuit, grabbed my board and paddled out into the thick kelp. The waves were small and oily. Fog was thick and everywhere. Seals swam just beyond the break.

The water was not like what is often seen in magazines and movies shot in California. It was a dreary and lonely experience with a forbidding feeling that loomed large on my Florida mind. The combination of the dense kelp, cold water, seals and fog left me without a single memory of any waves on that first morning. I do not remember being stoked. I do recall my mom waiting for me at the top of the cliff with a warm towel and a smile.

Life, like that first experience in the water of California, is not always full of stoke. Life is not always full of warm water, good waves, and sunshine. Sometimes all you can do is keep paddling, hoping that the surf gets better, and the wind turns offshore. But even if the surf does not get better, even if life is replete with rough spots and pain, frustration, and heartache —and it can be — surfing helps ease the anxiety. In this sense, surfing is a form of prayer. Surfing has the potential to release anxiety, fear, and hopelessness that can run as a thick thread through some of our days. Surfing focuses the mind and can sharpen the blade of hope. It takes you inside yourself, allowing for communion with God, a communion that pulses like the tides and borders on being sacramental.

Because surfing is all these things, and allows for all these things, I never cease to be amazed by the occasional guy — and it's always a guy — in the water with a foul attitude and a mouthful of invectives.

Not long ago on a Friday (my day off), the waves were as good as it gets in North Florida. The water was warm, the wind blowing just a few knots onshore. The waves were head high-plus with high water clarity. It was a spectacular day to be in the water. As I paddled out, I saw a guy on a shortboard whom I had never seen before catch a right and make a sweet and powerful cutback. The move was not perfect because he caught a rail but recovered. It was a beautiful ride. We paddled to the lineup, and I said to him, "Beautiful wave. Well surfed." He gave me a scowl like I had just cussed his mother. His face was hard and mean. "That wave sucked!" he said. "I F@#$% hate these waves! I can't surf worth a damn!"

Silently wondering if he was a sociopath, I paddled ahead and beyond him. I watched as he rode a good left, bailing off the back and screaming obscenities. I could not get far enough away from the man. The guy must have a miserable life at home, I thought. I was reminded that everyone is fighting an invisible battle. There are things that even surfing cannot heal. Still, I marvel at people like this shortboarder. The day was pristine, and we were surfing in the middle of the day when most people were working. We sat among porpoises with black-headed gulls flying overhead and pelicans dropping heavily from the sky, like brown thunderbolts. All this goodness and still the person could only see, hear, and feel anger. He may have been gliding on waves, but he did not know the mystery of the glide. I would venture to guess that he did not leave the water stoked, which is a form of blasphemy.

We exited the water at about the same time and as I watched him walk down the beach, I felt an emotion that reminded me of once seeing a dog right after it was hit by a car but not killed. The moaning and whimpering of the deeply pained.

22: Forgiveness

The English playwright Oscar Wilde quipped, "Always forgive your enemies—nothing annoys them so much." Wilde was right, of course. Though, we don't forgive someone for the sake of revenge, which is exactly what Wilde had in mind. No matter our intention, forgiveness is seldom an easy task. I suppose that's why the world's major religions put such an emphasis on practicing forgiveness. The "founders" of each religion or philosophy were wise enough to know that forgiveness does not come naturally and must be taught, reinforced, and taught again.

A jolting definition of forgiveness that I read came from Mark Twain: "Forgiveness is the fragrance that the violet sheds on the heel that has crushed it." Extending this metaphor, we might say that forgiveness is a form of love – the final form of love, according to Christian theologian Reinhold Niebuhr. But what exactly makes forgiveness so difficult? Why do most of us struggle to forgive people who have hurt us — or people who have hurt someone we love? It's difficult to forgive because when we opt to forgive, we opt out of blaming. When we forgive someone, we refuse to blame the one responsible for the injury. This is not to say that we may not hold the person responsible for his or her actions. But, rather, when we forgive, we excuse the offense done to us. And this is difficult precisely because when we excuse an offense, we give up the power, indeed even the thought, of revenge.

One of the reasons the world's great religions underscore the importance of forgiveness is each religion understands that without forgiveness of offenses it is impossible to live a life imbued with love. The longer we harbor thoughts of revenge, the longer we seek to blame someone for hurting us, the longer we live in the grip of hate and bitterness.

There is a story about a pastor in San Salvador who met an 11-year-old boy orphaned during El Salvador's civil war. A few years earlier, the boy had been rescued after his family was killed right in front of him. Somehow, he alone had survived the attack. Since the time his family was murdered, the boy spent entire days totally withdrawn, sometimes never speaking a word.

One day while the pastor was visiting the orphanage, the boy came to him and said, "Please pray for me, so that I can forgive the soldiers who killed my mother and brothers. I do not want to live with hatred in my heart." This 11- year-old boy was wise beyond his years. This boy somehow understood what hatred and bitterness could do to his heart. He intuited what theologian Lewis B. Smedes once wrote: "To forgive is to set a prisoner free and discover that the prisoner was you."

We all do the best we can with the tools we have. We all have baggage and emotional scars. We all have difficulties. Some of us, however, because of abuse or other trauma, live an existence that forever spirals downward.

Surfing is not a cure for every illness that impacts people grinding out a living. Surfing may not cure the shame of the 40-year-old restaurant server with two kids who wants more out of life, or the roofer who feels cheated by the American Dream, or the executive who feels she is imprisoned by golden handcuffs. Surfing cannot magically erase the pain of a man who has just lost his wife to cancer—but surfing can and does lighten life's burdens, even as it has the power to inflict bodily harm.

23: Injury

My first real in jury from surfing came when I was eighteen. It was the summer after my first Year at Flagler College. Tropical storm Alberto began as a depression north of Jacksonville, and as it moved northeast it generated an overhead exceptionally clean north swell. My roommate at the time was an old childhood friend named David who was living in St. Augustine during the summer. David and I rose early to check the waves. The waves were epic: well overhead and clean as a sheet of glass. The water was hot and there were just a few guys in the water.

We caught several gorgeous waves and we hooted at each other, stoked for each other's rides. The tubes were gaping and wide, almond shaped and large. Not long into the session, a set marched toward us, and I paddled to the horizon and over the first wave and second waves, spinning around to catch the final wave of the set. I was in a perfect position. Like God had sent me the wave. I took a couple of strokes, angling left, took off, slid down the face, grabbing my right rail with my right hand and dragging my left fingers in the wall of the wave to create balance and to slow my speed. I positioned myself for an enormous Florida tube. I distinctly recall the color of the wave as it came over me. It was light green, and I was covered in shadow. It was like being in a tent with a loud humming sound.

With the curtain of the wave obscuring the beach, I was deep in the tunnel, squarely placed for a beautiful glide. I marveled. For a split second I felt euphoria. The next second, I rode too high on the wall and got sucked up the face. I felt myself losing control, the board and myself no longer moving across the top of the glassy wall in a horizontal manner. The next thing I knew, I was upside down, being pitched forward and outward. The lip of the exploding curl drove me into the water, my board went free-flying, one of the fins slicing the corner of my eye – as close to the actual eyeball as one might get without cutting the eyeball. I felt the hit but did not think much of the impact.

Coming up out of the water, I took a breath, grabbed my leash, and pulled my board to where I floated. As I paddled back out, I felt a warming sensation on the right side of my face. Once back in the lineup, I reached up and put my fingers to the right side of my face. I took my hand away and saw blood. It covered my hand. I touched around my head and found the slice. Blood continued to run down my face, beginning to pool in the water next to my board. I called out to David who paddled over. "It looks bad," he said. He came closer and decided I should go to the hospital for stitches. I was out of the water for the remainder of the swell.

24: To Live is to Glide

Like most surfers who live near the beach, my daily routine involves an early morning call to one of my local surf shops to check the surf report. I check the wind. Check an online camera that will show me several breaks in St. Augustine. Sometimes I just ride the three blocks to the ocean to see for myself. This daily routine is etched on my heart. It's as natural as cracking open a beer after an evening surf session and lying in my hammock. It's as natural as telling my wife and son that I love them. For me, and countless others like me, to live is, in part, to glide. This is not to say that I could not or would not live without surfing because I have done both for extended periods of time. But the simple fact remains that while things have come and gone in my life, surfing has remained a constant.

The first time I went without regular surf sessions was when I moved to Colorado to conduct my own Thoreau-like experiment. Besides the obvious differences between my experiment and Thoreau's experiment (namely, he lived in Massachusetts in the 19th century), I did my experiment while living with a young woman and I did have electricity. Had Thoreau been given the opportunity to live with Ralph Waldo Emerson's wife, he would have jumped at the chance. To her credit, however, she did not reciprocate his love.

While living outside of Nederland, Vail, and Breckenridge, Colorado, for a combined total of twenty-two months, I found other pursuits involving nature and adrenaline. I tried my hand at rock climbing, skiing, downhill mountain biking, and some minor mountaineering. I enjoyed all these sports and they were good distractions from the glide — but they are not the glide.

I had other self-imposed exiles from surfing, though I would surf when I came home to Florida. One such exile took me to the mountains of North Carolina to learn the art of white water canoeing and to live on the New River, which I eventually paddled in total: from North Carolina to West Virginia. My time in North Carolina was marked by good times and good friends. The two other exilic periods from surfing include seminary in Atlanta and three years in western Virginia while serving my first parish. Even still, and long before the internet made wave updates so enticing with their photos, I would call the surf report, read magazines, and talk to friends who were still by the beach. When surfing is planted in your soul, when salt water is in your veins, life develops liquid handcuffs.

Not a day goes by that I don't at least call the surf report, exactly because rituals are the practice of meaning-making. Most days, not a day goes by that I don't ride my bike to the beach. There is something important to me about seeing the ocean. The ocean reminds me of my place — my spiritual geography — both emotionally and physically. As someone once said, "Tell me where you live, and I will tell you who you are."

25: Spiritual Practices

We all have spiritual practices, whether we know it or not. We have spiritual practices whether they are intentional or unintentional. Our daily lives suggest what we believe, what convictions we hold dear, what is worthy of our time, energy, resources, and love. We practice what we believe or want to believe. Or, conversely, we do not practice what we want to believe and, slowly over time, cease to believe what we hold dear. Our lives are infused with what our futures might become. What we do or don't do, believe, or do not believe comes to determine, in part, what our futures look like. While we do not have ultimate control over our lives — for life is largely beyond our control — we do have some degree of power over our choices. That helps to shape us into the people we will be, or not be, next year and in ten years.

Many of us live in an illusion of control. Many of us even live believing that we have some modicum of control over The Deity through prayers, promises, incantations, incense, or meditation. There is even an insidious movement in some Christian denominations that teach God will bless one with health or wealth: all you must do is believe and/or give more liberally of your resources. It's as if Jesus were a wealthy, healthy man who did not die penniless with a broken body. Theologically, you can't get more contrary to the historic and biblical teachings of Christianity than to confess a savior who wants you to be rich. To suggest that God wants me or you to be radically different from the incarnation of God is the heights of silliness.

There have been very few times when the subject of God or religion has surfaced while waiting for waves. The times when random spiritual conversations have arisen between myself and other surfers whom I do not know well are few. But I often talk of God, church, the Bible, and spiritual practices with people in the water whom I know well. Typically, however, the banter in the water is not serious. The conversations usually involve the current swell, a recent previous swell, or epic swells. Sometimes the conversation turns to where someone lives — and this thread is used to ferret out those who do not live in the vicinity of the break. All conversations in the water are fractured. One person will catch a wave and the conversation is put on pause, sometimes to be resumed and sometimes not. The heart of surfing does not involve communication. The heart is the glide.

26: Surfing is of God

Riding a wave down the line, whether making cutbacks or simply cruising, is the underpinning of the surfing experience. Whether right or left, riding on the face is the beginning point for all other aspects of the glide. Whether the wave is small or large, the line is the foundation. But, riding down the line is not the apex of surfing. Different waves produce different glides. Different surfers prefer different waves. Different conditions in the water — swell direction, wind, tide, bottom contour, size, moon phase — create different glides at the same break on the same day. Just as you can never step into the same ocean twice, neither can you ever ride the same wave twice. The glide is forever changing.

For example, not long-ago Hurricane Matthew ripped through St. Augustine Beach with buoys measuring thirty feet. My family and I evacuated, as did the entire population of our little island — except for those few people who chose to stay behind. We evacuated on a Thursday afternoon after sandbagging our garage and front door. We boarded all our east- facing windows with plywood. We packed as much as we could fit into our two cars and drove west to a Presbyterian Conference center some seventy-five miles inland. When we returned on Sunday morning, after the National Guard allowed us to cross the bridge to our home, I found the sandbar at my regular surf spot, FA, destroyed, rearranged, misshapen, and weird. My home break was a different break. The wave was unfamiliar. A dissimilar experience than the day before we evacuated. Before the hurricane, FA was a stable sandbar (oxymoron, yes), that had been producing a nice little wave on the right swell. But after the storm, the wave was disconnected with choppy sections, deep holes, and shallow dips.

Take this misshapen wave and then put a surface chop from a 10-knot wind and you have a wave that is not much fun, even at 13-second intervals. Riding the face of the wave is, of course, the heart of the glide. But on days that are choppy or when the form is unpredictable, riding the wave can be less than compelling. It can be frustrating. But it takes only one short glide to make the day. The stoke is found even in less-than-ideal circumstances. The stoke cannot be thwarted. If there is a glide, no matter how short or confused, the stoke remains. The glide is the stoke and the stoke is the glide. They are mystically paired and inseparable, which tells me that surfing was given by God.

In circumstances like these, the foundation of the glide might become something other than the glide. That is, surfing is more than the sum of its parts. While riding down the line is the foundation for the glide, the glide is but one part of the totality of the experience of surfing. On a day of bad waves, the foundation of the surf experience might be sitting in the lineup, watching the clouds as they appear and disappear, move, change in shape and color. Or, the foundation of the surf experience might be feeling the sun on your face, talking with a friend, feeling the breeze, enjoying the absence of people and human-created noise.

27: Beyond All

Surfing is both a bodily experience and an experience of the mind and or spirit. It is a holistic experience.

Surfing is a spiritual event. For surfers who hold to a belief in God, God often is encountered in the water. God might be sensed while waiting for a wave, talking with a friend in the lineup, watching a dolphin, or crouching like a cave dweller in a tube. God is found in the whole of the experience – especially in the moments of fear.

Honestly, though, to write that God is found in the whole experience of surfing may not be theologically accurate or philosophically sound. How does a person of limited mind and power find the invisible, mysterious, cosmic force known as God? Such talk of finding God – as if God is like a lost key that we have somehow misplaced – is bound up with hubris. One cannot find God. But one might be found by the invisible, mysterious, cosmic force known as God. So, it is God who does the finding of a surfer who waits for a wave. It is God who finds a surfer who watches a tarpon roll. It is God who finds a surfer in a barrel. We can no more find God than a bird can fly to the moon. We can only be found. While we may be seekers, we are not finders. We may look, practice, and believe, but our actions are a moot point if God does not want to be found. And if God wants to be found then it is God who does the finding. We are always the recipients of discovery. We are not discoverers. And though it is true that we can make ourselves more open to experiencing God through prayer, meditation, and other exercises, our spiritual disciplines, while working on our receptiveness to mystery through a quietness of mind, do not automatically inform us of God. There's no dynamic equivalent between praying and intuiting God. God can't be intuited unless God wants to be intuited by the one praying. God is, by definition, beyond all.

28: Desert

I once spent several weeks in the desert on the border between Texas and Mexico. It was more dazzling than I had expected. Very open and very rough. Different shades of brown. Quiet beyond comprehension. The quiet was so stark that it spooked me. At the beginning of my time in the desert, I thought something was always hiding behind the silence. Quietness is like that. Real, deep quietness brings a person in contact with a sense of nothingness: and that can be terrifying. But I loved the quiet, the nothingness. There are many days that I now hunger for what I didn't hear in the desert, days when I think of the absolute stillness. The Psalmist writes, "Be still and know that I am God." The desert is quiet enough to hear God listening to the world. The desert is also quiet enough to hear your own thoughts as they take shape. The desert can be without sound in such a way that it's possible to hear what no sound sounds like. The closest I have ever come to hearing this kind of silence outside the desert is while surfing a large, long-period period swell in the very early morning.

Four years after graduating from Flagler College, I went to the desert. It was Christmas and I was alone, more than 1,500 miles away from my family in Florida. Christmas, and I was camped in an isolated site on Terlingua Creek in the Big Bend of Texas, which is also called the Borderland. Surrounding me were giant mesas filling the distant reaches of the sky and reddish peaks that reminded me of red brick steeples. A desolate country.

It was Christmas morning, and I was sad. I was feeling sorry for myself and yet, at the same time I felt excellent and free. I also felt very close to the earth, which is almost always a good feeling. I woke to the sound of coyotes. Their cries were shrill. Their barks had a dream-like quality to them. I listened to them and then remembered that I had three Christmas presents in my possession, which had been mailed to me by my mom. I had picked them up at a post office in Austin, Texas, and saved these presents to open on Christmas morning. The wrapping paper on all three presents was red. Inside one of the gifts was a large card that I had colored for my parents when I was seven years old. When I saw the card, a symbol of love, I cried. At that moment, I hated my freedom and wanted to be with family in Florida.

Freedom, like silence, is like that; it is paradoxical. Freedom is a double-edged sword. It is liberty but it also can be bondage.

The weather on that Texas Christmas morning was clear and warm. It reminded me of Florida weather in the winter. The air was dry, and I slept well. I felt sad, but I felt free. There is nothing in this life quite as beautiful as a sense of freedom, by which I mean, freedom from commitments and responsibilities. My sense of freedom grew every time I stared into the distance, a distance that never seemed to end but continued with a copper earth that eventually ran into a thin stretch of blue sky. I think that's one reason I like the dessert: it is like the horizon while surfing. An endless nothing except nature. There really is no way for me to communicate how free I felt. I don't think I will ever feel that way again because that brand of

71

freedom may not faithfully coexist with Christian faith. The freedom I felt was a freedom fueled by selfish anti-ambition.

Being alone in the desert was like being alone waiting for a wave, which often produces self-reflection in me. In the desert I found myself asking, "Who am I? What do I stand for?" The desert silenced all answers. Indeed, the silence was the answer. Appreciation of quietude is a virtue lost upon our culture, which is even more reason to acquire this virtue. Love of silence may not help someone invest money, but it will help to invest your soul.

I had come to the desert to do all the things, and more, which people do for recreation in the desert. I had come to hike and climb, watch birds and sunsets and appreciate the vast amount of silence. I also went to meditate alone for an entire month, but this got interrupted when I fell in with a large group of people who were camping on the Rio Grande for several weeks. My month of silent meditation and contemplation became a mixture of aloneness and one large, nonstop party with the group. We imbibed in everything natural and good and illegal, barely escaping arrest for certain activities after a few of us were caught coming back from Mexico where we were ferried across the river by a young boy in a makeshift boat with a long pole who beached us stateside as six Border Patrol Officers had a photo taken by a journalist for a story on the War on Drugs.

I went to the desert with the sole intention of listening for something like God, though at that time in my life I had stopped believing much in God. Over the course of my month, I did not hear God speak, but I did find incredible stillness. God is not necessarily to be found in places, per se, though some places do seem to make it easier to commune with God —

places like the desert or ocean. But God is in all places, the still desert as much as a crowded and chaotic city. In both places, the desert and the ocean, I have found joy, which is given by God. And this joy that is given by God is found especially in good waves. While we may not have the power to find God, we do have some amount of power to find good waves, which can lead to immense joy and deep consideration of the God who gives joy. Surfers differ on what makes a great wave. But we all know joy. For some, a great wave might be Pipeline in Hawaii. For others, it might be the uncrowded, chilly water of Oregon. For others, like me, it might be warm water, head-high waves at a local sandbar during the month of October.

29: October

October is Florida's best opportunity for waves of consistent quality and size. The continued possibility for tropical cyclones — tropical storms and hurricanes — still exists and there is the added possibility for northeasters, though often these storms are close period wind swells. In October, the water temperature is still warm to mild (high to low seventy's) and the sun is still strong. The crowds of summer vacationers have returned to their homes and the snowbirds have not yet flown south.

In October, the likelihood of a good swell on a regular basis is at its zenith. We had two such swells last October. Both were head to overhead high with light, variable winds. Both swells peaked during the work week. The water was in the high seventies and the only crowds were locals and kids from Flagler College. For me, this is surfing at its best. Good waves at home with clear, warm water, a friend or two, and few people surfing. This is not to say that I don't like to travel to distant lands in search of great waves. But my truth is that of Dorothy's in *The Wizard of Oz*: "There is no place like home." Is it great to surf beautiful waves in far flung places? Of course. But home is home and for many people, like me, home is the foundation and ground of what is good, and true, and meaningful. If home is not the ground of what is good, true, and meaningful, then home has not yet been found. Can home be found on the road while searching for waves? Maybe. But the road is not reality, in the sense of what defines a home. The road is fantasy. I have made enough trips to know this to be true. The road is a state of mind that does not need to consider a continual, responsible existence. This is not to say that travel puts one above morality. Only that travel, by its very nature, is movement. When you travel you are not at home? You are moving either away from home or toward home. And while travel is stupendous, it cannot give you a firm social location. Only home can do that.

30: The Road

In my early twenties, I lived like a gypsy for several years. I traveled all over the western United States. I carried everything I owned in a backpack. I slept in canyons, hitchhiked through deserts, surfed in mythic places, took Greyhound buses (a must for gritty, cheap, travel), and slept in strangers' homes. I knew the road. I felt threatened in Colorado by a delusional guy who gave me a ride outside of Vail, and barely escaped being murdered next to the bus station in downtown Atlanta at 1 a.m. I was shot at outside of Bolinas, California, for sleeping in a rancher's pasture, which forced me to a coffee shop outside of Point Reyes. There, I met a young lady who gave me a bed, homemade brownies, and eventually a ride to San Francisco to surf. I know the road.

And while the road is not reality, it is a reality, only not the reality that most of us aspire to permanently attain. Travel is its own version of what is real. And for me that doesn't have any resemblance to home. So, when I say that for me surfing at its best is gliding on excellent October waves at my home break, I mean to say that there is no wave like one's home break. The home break is part of what makes home, home. The glide that happens on a good day at your home break is what helps to make home beautiful, true, and meaningful.

I have not taken a lot of surf trips outside of Florida. Last count around fifteen. I have never been to Indonesia. Never been to Fiji. Am I the worst for it? I don't know. Do I care? No. Why? Because I have been to other places throughout the world. Would I like to go to Fiji and Indonesia? Absolutely. But I don't lose sleep over not surfing those world-class waves. Why? Because I have my home break. In other words, I am content. Contentment, to some important degree, is what fuels the love of home. Without contentment, home cannot be home.

This is not to say that some days while swinging in my hammock with a beer I don't think back to the north shore of Kauai. I recall the power of the waves. The aqua color of the water. The long paddle out at Hanalei Bay. The beautiful right-hander that rolls over a living reef sparked by color. I recall the hard-hitting sandbar at Pine Trees that was thick with surfers and a fast wave. There are days swinging in my hammock that I think back to the Princeville wave. Walking the steep and rocky path to the beach, which is lined with basalt-looking rock, palm trees, and flowers of every variety. And I remember only a few guys out, all nice, all helpful. I remember the wave almost double overhead and so strong and steep that my mini-gun had trouble making the drop.

When I think back to Kauai, I recall chickens. Everywhere. The roosters crowing at 5 a.m., wrecking my jet lagged rest, their crowing cutting through sliding glass doors and making its way into my sleep. The best thing about Kauai is the waves. The second-best thing would be dead roosters.

My wife and I stayed on the north shore, in Princeville, for eight days in October of 2008. Every morning when I returned from surfing, I would grab some coffee, sit on the back porch and long for a BB gun. Give me a day, I thought, and I could make a dent in this paradise. The chickens and roosters on the north shore of Kauai are sacred cows. No touching allowed. Certainly, no BB guns.

31: FA

On the island that I live on, Anastasia, we do not, thankfully, let chickens run amok or roosters roam freely. At one time in the not-too-distant past, there were chickens walking freely in one neighborhood on the south end of St. Augustine Beach. It's said that someone shot them with BB guns. I swear it wasn't me. What we do have on Anastasia Island, however, and something every coastal area in my native state has and struggles with is over development. I've read, but have not confirmed, that Florida has lost more forested land, as a total percentage, than any other state in the U.S. I have also read and do believe that the population of the Florida east coast has doubled in the last 30 years.

My home break, FA, has witnessed the development of a massive Embassy Suites Hotel on the beach, which was built on the politics of redirection and deception. It is the northern most piece of development directly on the beaches of Anastasia Island. Gratefully, the three miles that extend to the north on the island are owned by the Florida State Park system. For three miles there is nothing but sand dunes and shells. Nothing but sand all the way to the inlet that separates St. Augustine Beach from Vilano Beach.

Years ago, it was possible to drive on the beach owned by the Florida State Park system. But then, as accidents happen, a guy ran over two girls sunbathing. At that time, people were of two minds: condemn the driver but don't close the beach to vehicles. When the park decided to close the beach to vehicular traffic, I wasn't happy. It's a rather long haul to surf breaks such as Blowhole and Middles. Now, because no vehicles are allowed on the beach, the surf spots are mostly empty. The beach is without litter. There is no visual pollution. Today, I am grateful for the park's decision to disallow driving on the beach in Anastasia State Park. Today, I can walk for three miles among the gulls, terns, and sand pipers and hear nothing except the wind and waves. There is no construction to ruin the beachscape. This is good for the soul.

32: Imagination

There are many things that are good for the soul, by which I mean activities or no activity that gives life and newness, a respite from the daily grind on a person's imagination and hope. Imagination and hope are towering figures in our lives, even when, or especially when, we don't recognize our need for them. Imagination is, by my reckoning, the faculty given by God that propels us forward, physically, scientifically, artistically, emotionally, and spiritually. Hope feeds the imagination, and without hope, the imagination would die. We need only look at Sylvia Plath, Ernest Hemmingway, Jim Morrison, or Kurt Cobain to see this truth. Loss of hope can lead to loss of life, though often the loss of hope leads to a person living a life of quiet desperation, to paraphrase Henry David Thoreau.

33: Costa Rica

In 2010 I made my second, and to date, last solo trip to Costa Rica. Over the years, several people have told me that they find it odd that I would do not one, but two solo surf trips to Central America. While traveling alone, lodging alone, eating alone, and not speaking much to anyone for an entire week strikes many people as odd, there is a logic to my madness. If I cannot find someone to surf with that I really want to be with, I would rather be alone than poorly accompanied. Over the years, I have come to enjoy, and appreciate (if that isn't too bold to say) my own company. And so, in 2010 I went to CR by myself, my best surfing buddy, Joe, unable to go that year.

To make the trip easy, relaxing, and virtually free of any stress, I flew direct from Orlando to San Jose, the Jet Blue plane crowded with eco-tourists and middle-aged offshore anglers from all over the U.S. The plane descended over the mountains that resemble scoops of furry green ice cream, a light brown cloud hung over the city and valley, large chunks of forest stripped from the earth to make room for an ever-expanding economy. In this way, Costa Rica always reminded of Florida. Once I landed and retrieved my board, I found a man in a red T-shirt and blue jeans outside the terminal, whose name was Jose'. Jose' stood statue-like with a sign reading, "Hunter Camp." He grabbed my duffel bag and we walked to the garage and got in his white van with double sliding doors. He lit a cigarette.

Jose's English was infinitely better than my Spanish and so we conversed as we made our way through the sprawl of San Jose and its diesel-clogged roadways. From there we picked up Route 1 and headed south to 27/721 past San Antonio, Concepcion, Escobal. We skirted the River Tarcoles continuing south past Coyolar to 34 South, which led us near the outermost and southeastern edge of the Carara National Park. We passed a couple of restaurants perched at the edges of various cliffs offering spectacular views of the valley below. We passed billboard after billboard, 95 percent of which were in English advertising the next great development with the next great pool and the next great spa. We passed roadside vendors selling authentic and inauthentic wares, fruit, Coke made from sugar cane, and one booth with coconuts.

Not long after driving through the national park, off to the distant right, the Iguana Golf Course could be seen. Shortly after the golf course is the left turn to Jaco Beach, which was to be my home base for the week. Jaco Beach is located on the Central Pacific side of the country, lying between Herradura to the north and Hermosa Beach to the south. Jaco Beach is a small, dirty, nastier Daytona Beach where drugs are easily sold on the sidewalks and where families of Americans and Europeans stroll before and after dinner, bumping elbows with prostitutes. It is not quaint. I lodged in the southern part of the town, closer to Hermosa Beach, which is not as touristy or as gritty.

Costa Rica has changed dramatically since my first surf trip in 1989. Back then, even San Jose was slow. I recall seeing a donkey pull a cart down the main boulevard. But now, any such donkeys would be run over and killed by 20-wheel trucks. The drive from San Jose to Jaco Beach, in 1989, took us about five hours. Only eighty-eight kilometers in five hours. Today, that same route can be made in just over an hour and a half. In 1989, Jaco Beach had one hotel, which is still in existence. The roads were dirt. The people kind. Back then, a small room on the beach without air conditioning or hot water, but with a fan, cost $3 per night. Back then it was paradise, which is exactly why it is no longer paradise. The paradise has become a hub for seedy money from South American mobsters and North American expats with beer bellies and gold chains, strutting around like roosters who need their wings clipped.

34: Arrogance

Not long ago, I was at a gathering with other clergy. And, as I mingled among my colleagues of different religious traditions, Christian and non-Christian, I came upon one man who, when introducing himself, told me how large, rich, and well established his congregation happens to be. He went on to brag about his accomplishments and attempted to educate me on my own tradition. I found myself wondering, "Is this guy for real? Are we on Candid Camera? Does this man realize how pompous he is?"

Pomposity, of course, is not limited to members of the clergy. Arrogance is not limited to the religiously inclined among us. But this we can say: arrogance is a sign of fear and insecurity. And experience has shown me that the Judeo-Christian text from Proverbs is true: "Pride comes before destruction and an arrogant spirit before the fall."

I'm not immune to arrogance. My wife will tell you as much. Nevertheless, the clergyman I mentioned above would do well to take advice from the 12th century Muslim theologian, Al-Ghazali: "Declare your jihad (Holy War) on 13 enemies you cannot see — egoism, arrogance, conceit, selfishness, greed, lust, intolerance, anger, lying, cheating, gossiping and slandering."

As with many things in life, arrogance is a condition of the heart. A spiritual condition. The more you feed the ego, the more arrogant you become. And the more arrogant you become, the more estranged from God you will become. Arrogance is the desire to live in a world of fantasy — a self-made world, rather than a God-made world. Sometimes the best we can do is to learn that we must struggle to become less arrogant and less haughty. And if we think for a second that we are not arrogant or haughty, that is an arrogant thought itself.

There is an old story about a Cherokee grandfather telling his grandson about the struggle between good and bad that happens within us all. The granddaddy said the struggle is between two wolves. One wolf was evil: Anger, envy, greed, arrogance, self-pity, gossip, resentment, and false pride. The other was good: Joy, peace, love, hope, serenity, humility, kindness, generosity, truth, compassion, and faith. The grandson thought about it for a moment and then asked his grandfather, 'Which wolf do you think will win?' The old Cherokee replied, 'The wolf that you feed.'

35: Beer Before Lunch

J ose' drives us through Jaco Beach, Costa Rica, a town that has become like so many before it: spoiled. Spoiled to my vacationing eyes but not spoiled to the many Ticans who have risen above poverty due to the massive influx of eco-tourists and ex-pats. And yet, to even some of the Ticans, it has become what it never was before.

One incident brought this feeling home to me. I was surfing down around Dominical in 2006. I exited the water and walked past a cadre of women and young girls having a picnic on the dark sand, seated on a baby blue blanket underneath the shade of a tree stand. In my rudimentary Spanish, I wished them, "Hello, and good day," only to be met with a venomous response from the elderly matriarch of the clan. She responded by telling me, "Go back north. Leave my country." It chilled me to the bone. And I thought, just because a thing is good for business, just because a thing brings economic development, does make that thing just or moral or healthy. Economics is not the highest good and the only rubric to measure wellbeing.

Jose' continued driving through Jaco Beach, past the trinket shops selling shell souvenirs made in the Philippines and Indonesia. Past the fast food and bars. Past the park with a few shade trees and a yellow park bench. Past the pretentious Quicksilver shop and the myriad of surf shops, fishing charters, massage parlors, and bikinis. I think back to the time when I drove this same road when it was dirt and there were no shops, only a couple of open-air places to eat. We make it to the southern end of the strip, driving past a brown-skinned child wearing a Miami Dolphins shirt that is too large for him.

When we get to where the road splits, Jose bears right just past the Pentecostal church, which is the fastest-growing branch of Christianity in Latin America. We drive a short distance, a quarter of a mile, and take a right under the arch onto the grounds of the hotel, which is not very grand, and we snake our way back to the old and low-slung units, pull up to the brown-walled guest check-in, and I hop out, grab my board and duffle, and say goodbye to Jose.

I spent the next five days catching decent waves right behind the hotel, never needing to venture far afield. The waves varied from chest high to well overhead. In the morning, the water was mostly glassy, the wind calm or slightly offshore. The form was fair, sometimes almost good. Never excellent. Every morning, after a two-hour surf I'd head in for breakfast, then grab a book and lie on the beach, under a palm, or by the pool, sometimes having a beer before lunch.

36: Stingray

O n the fifth day, in the late afternoon, after surfing the worst waves of the trip, I caught a long right and decided to make it my last wave of the day. I took the wave all the way to the beach. I stepped off my board to walk the few feet toward the sand. And then I felt it, like glass or a nail or sharp metal. I thought the glass, nail, or sharp metal had pierced my right heel. I stopped, just shy of the beach, and hobbled onto the sand. With each step the pain increased exponentially. Once on the sand I lifted my heel to have a look. A small puncture oozing blood. Nothing major. But a bluish-blackish shade around the small hole had begun to form at the edges of my heel. The pain became excruciating. And then I knew what I did not want to know. A stingray.

Every surfer and saltwater angler learn to be wary of the stingray, which is a cartilaginous fish akin to sharks. Its barbed tail is used in self-defense and can reach lengths of fourteen inches. The stinger is covered with a thin skin-like substance where venom is stored and the barbs at the end of the stinger inject the venom. There are over two hundred distinct species of stingrays, ranging from deep cold-water rays to shallow-dwelling tropical species. Deaths from stingray venom are rare. But, in 2006, Steve "Crocodile

Hunter" Irwin was in Australia's Great Barrier Reef, when he was stuck by a stingray in his thoracic wall, killing him. And though death is rare from stingrays, the pain is exceptionally strong. I have heard it said that the pain caused by a stingray is as close as a man ever gets to the pain of natural childbirth.

Years after my encounter with the stingray in Costa Rica, I was fishing off a bulkhead in the Keys. A large man, the size of a bull, fully covered with tattoos on his neck and chest, began fishing next to me. We talked like men who are strangers sharing a common moment. The conversation turned to stingrays. We exchanged stories of being stung. The man said to me, "Worse than being stabbed or shot. Got stabbed in prison and got shot before going to prison. The damn ray is worse." The man's admission of the pain confirmed my own experience that my pain from the ray was worse than broken bones and torn ligaments. I was not being a sissy when I hobbled from the water and could barely make it back to my room at the hotel.

I stood at the water's edge for a moment to collect my thoughts and to process the situation. It's not glass. Not a nail. A ray. I limped like a three-legged dog to my room. The walk was no more than one hundred meters. Not far. But I could barely make it. Didn't think I could make it. I hobbled past the bar and the pool and sun worshippers. My face was sweating, my jaw clenched. I dropped my board on the hard, Mexican tile floor, cranked the A/C and closed the curtains before crawling into bed. I faced the ceiling. The pain continued to grow. I was both astounded at the severity and worried that it would not end. The burning sensation in my foot began to spread upward and soon my calf was burning. It felt fire was inside the muscle. I was amazed at the acuteness of the pain. The fire inside my calf quickly spread to my knee then to my quad and not long after, reached my groin. The entire lower half of my torso felt like it was being bathed in flames.

I thought I might be having an allergic reaction to the toxin of the stingray. In the darkened room my mind wandered to my wife and young son at home in Florida. I began to wonder if I would die when the venom found my lungs or heart. I was chilled, shaking. My muscles were cramping.

I felt nauseous and faint. My heart rate soared. I thought I would die in that bed. I wanted to get help, but to move and put weight on my right leg seemed impossible. When the burning hit my stomach, I willed myself out of the bed and out of the room. "I must get help," I thought to myself. "I don't want to die in this room."

Whether or not I would have died from the stingray venom I will never know. But that is beside the point. The feeling of imminent death, whether real or imagined, surely has a similar psychological impact as well as a neurological impact. And so, I hopped and limped to the guest check-in where I summoned the manager, explained my situation, then collapsed onto a couch. A cab was called and showed up a few minutes later. I felt as if I was in a dream – hazy, and uncertain. The manager helped me to the car, the cab driver eased me in, and the manager got in with me, directing the driver to hurry to the pharmacy. The manager made a call on his cell. I do not remember the ride. I remember being helped by the two men into the pharmacy where a lengthy line of locals waited for medication. The pharmacist, who has broader medical powers than pharmacists in the U.S, waved us back to a private room. He wasted no time: "Remove your pants.

Bend over." I watched as the man grabbed a shot with the longest needle I had ever seen. It looked like a sword Lancelot might have carried into battle.

I did as he said. He jabbed me with the needle. He sat back in a creaky wooden chair. "Bad sting. You feel better very soon." He shuffled me out of the semi-private room, handing me off to the manager and cab driver who walked me to the car. Within minutes of getting in the car, I felt better. The skin around my heel and ankle, however, would take months to heal. There was significant tissue necrosis.

37: Storms of Life

Eckhart Tolle, a popular spiritual writer influenced by Zen Buddhism, Sufism, Hinduism, and the Bible wrote, "Whenever something negative happens to you, there is a deep lesson concealed within it." I don't know if this is always true. But Tolle's opinion is found in many of the world religions. And this opinion is a good rule to follow when life presents dark moments, challenging times, and pain.

In his book, Finding God in the Dark, David Walls writes about Presbyterian minister Dr. Lloyd John Ogilvie, and the struggles he had in his first year as the U.S. Senate Chaplain. In the previous year, his wife had undergone five major surgeries, radiation treatment and chemotherapy. Several key staff teammates moved on to other assignments, which added pressure and uncertainty to Ogilvie's work. Problems that he could have tackled with gusto under normal circumstances seemed to loom in all directions. Discouragement lurked around every corner. Prayer was no longer a contemplative luxury, but the only way to survive. Wall's quotes Ogilvie:

"My own intercessions were multiplied by the prayers of others. Friendships were deepened as I was forced to allow people to assure me with words I had preached for years. No day went by without a conversation, letter or phone call giving me love and hope."

Ogilvie's story is a reminder that when we find ourselves in the storms of life, God is still present. It also reminds me that a deep prayer life and an ability to turn to others for help go a long way toward making the pain bearable. Through prayer and through the care of others, God's peace can strengthen us during life's most pressing times.

Surfing is, by its very nature, a solo activity. You don't need a team, in most circumstances, to accomplish the glide. But surfing has been a communal practice. Surfing has communities of people who gravitate to one another to talk about waves. I don't know whether surfers are better or worse at turning to others for help in times of need. I do know, however, that surfers often come together to celebrate and help their own in times of trouble and in crises.

Former head of the United Nations, Dag Hammarskjold, wrote about his own journey through life's pain. Hammarskjold suffered three years of intense darkness in his life – a time of anguish and inner turmoil. And somehow, in some way, God met him in the darkness of his night. He wrote, "At some moment I did answer "Yes" to Someone – or Something – and from that hour I was certain that existence is meaningful and that, therefore, my life had a goal."

Many people look back with regret on dark moments in their life, but Hammarskjold understood that God used that time to break into his life with new meaning, hope, and redemption. In other words, he understood that a deep lesson was concealed within times of anguish—exactly because God is present within all our experiences, but especially in the darkest times of our lives.

As it relates to God, prayer, hope, and meaning, I'm still not entirely sure what to make of my stingray experience. Maybe it doesn't relate at all. More probably, the experience does relate to God and prayer, hope and meaning. That's because all of life relates to these elements, which comprise the very stuff of human existence. The experience of the stingray does suggest that surfing has a unique component that lends itself to greater risk for pain. Part of the glide is encountering danger. Part of the glide, if you do it long enough, is injury.

The idea that there is pain in a God-filled world has long perplexed theologians. Questions often go like this: "Why would God – supposing that this God is all good, just, and loving – allow pain and suffering among the creatures that this God creates?" "What benefit is there to God, or the world, which justifies the existence of pain?" "Why does evil exist?" "Why is there poverty, warfare, and disease?" "Why does a good God allow car accidents and cancer?"

Questions and concerns such as this fall under a theological doctrine called theodicy. But no amount of thinking about these questions, no amount of biblical research, or research into texts outside of the Bible, will produce any answers — or, at least, any answers that satisfy people who are beset with pain or evil. The old and tired response, "God has to allow for evil, without which good would not be good," is pat, and if true, not highly creative on the part of God. Or "God gave humans free will, and some people choose to abuse their power." This is a quaint Sunday School answer and, if true, suggests a problem, not with free will, but with the God who created free will. Besides this, answers such as the ones I just mentioned are simple theological rejoinders not worthy of God, or of those who suffer. For me, the most satisfying answer to the problem of evil is simply: "Ultimately speaking, I don't know why evil exists and I don't know why people suffer." Anything beyond these words becomes conjecture. Th existence of evil reminds us that we live in a world of unknowns.

38: The Ocean

To surf is to glide into the unknown. The ocean is beyond absolute predictability. To surf is to move among mystery, which is why surfing is at heart a spiritual practice, even if the one surfing does not understand the activity as spiritual. To surf is to embrace a dualism of sorts: that is, the surfing life (like life in general), is filled with good days of surf and bad days of surf.

The surfing life has moments of extreme joy and extreme pain. This is obvious to those who surf, but that doesn't indicate a lack of mystery inherent in the glide, or that the glide is built upon the obvious. There are certainties implicit in surfing, but these certainties comprise only three elements: the surfer, the board, and the wave. Some may argue that a particular wave is predictable and certain, which to a degree may be true. But, as any seasoned waterman will tell you, nothing in the wiles of the ocean is certain. The ocean is too complex, too full of energy to be reduced to certainty. And, to an important degree, so is surfing. Surfers do not define surfing, but the other way around. Surfing defines us. The glide is beyond a simple definition, which is why we are defined by the glide.

In our scientifically, mechanized North American culture, there is a high value placed upon known quantities and qualities. We place enormous emphasis on certainty, on what can be expected when "A encounters B." We like predictability because predictability lures us into believing that we are safe and secure, that things are known, if not always easy and anodyne. And while there is nothing wrong with predictability or comfort, if these qualities come to define us, or become masters of our lives, then mystery will be consumed by certainty. And if everything in life becomes certain, then life takes on a waif-like quality. A vapor. A shadow. Life is no longer life but a managed artifice.

Surfing embraces uncertainty. Even the overly sponsored kid bragging about his latest maneuver retains a measure of the mystery of the glide because he or she knows that the ocean is unpredictable. Because the ocean is unpredictable, so, too, is surfing. The same might be said about God and those who worship this God. That is, even fundamentalists who believe the Bible is inerrant and that every comma and period found in the King James translation was divinely appointed (though the Greek and Hebrew of the Bible are missing such punctuation), even still, these believers traffic in mystery.

39: The Bible

When I was sixteen, I believed the Bible to be historically factual from beginning to end. Without errors. I believed many things to be certain and did not feed on mystery.

The ground I stood upon was solid. Everything was firm and settled. Faith questions were not my friends —questions, foundational questions about the veracity of a biblical story or biblical text, did not enter my life until my first year of college.

I used to believe many things, but now I believe fewer things. But I believe these fewer things with greater depth. I have come to the tentative conclusion that right belief (orthodoxy) is not as important as I once believed it to be. Today, right action (orthopraxy) seems more consequential, and biblical, to the well-being of the world than right belief, however one chooses to define right belief. To paraphrase Martin Luther, a wise Muslim is preferred as a ruler than a foolish Christian.

40: Timing

It was not yet light when I paddled out. The buoys were reading 13 seconds at 5'. A good, solid swell. Along the beach, the waves looked to be head-high plus. The water was still with an oily-calm surface. A few young grommets were already in the lineup. I made it to the mid-bar with my hair still dry and began to stroke hard for the horizon. I timed it wrong. The first wave broke just in front of my longboard, and I tried to turtle — flip over and hang on tight underwater — but the wave ripped the board from my hands and sent me spinning into the warm foamy water. I came up, took a quick breath and the second wave cracked, exploding on my head, sending me deep, spinning me head over feet. My leash stretched and pulled at my right ankle. I relaxed and let the wave roll me around. My breath became thin, and I found the surface, sucking in foam and a hint of air before the third wave, bigger than the other two, crashed just beyond me, giving me time to dive deep, away from the turbulence. I felt the stirrings of fear as my oxygen began to run out. I felt the burn in my chest and my head began to pound.

There have been many such occasions in my life and the life of surfers I know. That moment when you think to yourself, "If I don't get air right now, I'm in deep trouble." Or, just as scary, the moment when you surface after the third wave to see a fourth wave in the set getting ready to pound you. The experience of running out of oxygen with no immediate way to take in oxygen doesn't often happen in places like Florida. But it does happen, every now and then, and can catch us off guard. The moment a surfer begins to believe that the ocean, no matter the swell size, is completely safe, that is the moment when tragedy can strike. Typically, on a well-groomed, spread-out swell one can time the sets and paddle out relatively unscathed. I have paddled dry-headed to the outside lineup more times than I can count. In the eighth century BC, the Greek poet Hesiod wrote, "Observe due measure, for right timing is in all things the most crucial factor." This maxim is as true in surfing as it is in love and war. And yet, as hard as we surfers may try, our timing comes and goes. While we may be relative experts in timing, we learn through the years that there are days when, no matter how we may try, our timing is off and there's precious little we can do about it.

Timing is crucial to the glide — to its setup, paddling, standing up, drawing the best line, bottom turns, tube riding, and knowing when to kick out and get off the wave. Timing is about judgment and reflexes but something even more mystical: intuition. Judgment and timing take patience and practice. Intuition is not so easily earned or discovered. The saying, "The one who hesitates is late," is true in surfing, and if you are late —if your timing is off — it is more likely that the nose of your board will penetrate the surface of the water and send you head over heels. Or, even worse, hesitation causes you and your board to go over the falls, sucked into the cascading curl that is the breaking wave, which then pummels you for poor judgment.

In many places like Florida, there is usually no great harm done to the surfer who takes off late and finds himself or herself being pitched outward and downward by a lack of timing. In most cases, the waves are not big enough or powerful enough to inflict severe damage. But in locations all around the world there are waves breaking on coral and rock reefs, or large waves breaking on shallow sandbars, where a late takeoff or poor judgment can make the difference between life and death — and everything in between.

41: Late Take Off

The first time I took off late on a coral reef break was in Barbados. I was surfing just off the famous break called Soup Bowls. It was January of 1989. There were few guys out because the waves were not exceptionally clean. But the waves were large enough to put a VW Bug in the barrel. I remember taking off right and hesitating because of fear. I did not push myself to get into the wave but held back ever so slightly because I feared what could happen if I did not make the wave. And that is what often makes the difference between a successful take-off and a wipeout. The judgment. The timing. The intuition. And the grip of fear that can tower over all other emotions, thoughts, and reason itself.

As I took off on the wave, I knew immediately that I had made a wrong decision. No way was I going to make the drop. I was too late. And I was too late because I hesitated. My feet touched the board as the board shifted sideways, the right rail not firmly planted in the face of the wave. I was thrown into the trough — the place where the wave breaks. Because of my sorry position on the wave, I was quickly and forcefully pushed to the reef below. My left shoulder hit the coral and then my left knee. Surfacing, and making it to the beach, I learned a vital lesson: Do. Not. Hesitate. Either go, or do not go. Hesitation is often the difference between failure and success.

42: Failure

If there is one thing that is endemic to humanity, it is failure. Failure is universal. There are more or less successful people; but all people have endured failure. Failure happens in politics, morality, sports, business, academics, or taking off on a wave. Failure happens in relationships, or it may happen with one's own integrity. Regardless, no one lives without tasting the bitter fruit of failure.

According to the late psychologist B.F. Skinner, "A failure is not always a mistake; it may simply be the best one can do under the circumstances. The real mistake is to stop trying." I suppose we have all heard something along these lines from parents, teachers, friends, or clergy. "Don't give up," they say. So we push forward, trusting that, as someone once said, "Our best successes often come after our greatest disappointments."

When it comes to surfing, it's hard to determine exactly what constitutes failure. Of course, there's the obvious failure of not making a wave and wiping out. That's a specific and isolated failure. But what would happen if surfers strung together all the wipeouts and missed opportunities we encounter in the water? Would we consider ourselves failures — in a larger, more existential sense of the word? When does one's life become a failure? What is the measuring stick or rubric for a failed life? Is there, or can there be, a universal determination of such a thing? I think not. So much of our life — and our surfing — is tied to context. While Postmodernism has given rise to many ills in Western culture, I celebrate the freedom that this paradigm has brought to the idea of success. For too long success has been equated with the unhealthy ideal that involves and often revolves around making a lot of money.

Sometimes our highest hopes are destroyed so that we can be prepared for better things. Our failures can be the door to a new success. As the Yogi, Paramahansa Yogananda, wrote, "The season of failure is the best time for sowing the seeds of success.

It's usually assumed Handel's "Messiah" was written at the pinnacle of his success. But that's not the case. The composition was written after Handel suffered a stroke and had suffered through a particularly desperate night of despair over his failure as a musician. Upon waking, Handel unleashed his creative genius in a musical score that continues to inspire us generations later. Failure happens. But so does success.

People often give up after one or two attempts at something in which they have failed (such as taking off late on a wave in Barbados in hopes of getting a sick tube). But success often comes after multiple failed attempts. If I had given up surfing after only a few tries because I judged my success and failure by what is possible in surfing, then my life would look very different today. I would not be writing this book. I wouldn't have had certain key experiences that have made me into the man that I am today. As Thomas Edison remarked about the continual problems related to his invention of the light bulb: "I have not failed. I've just found 10,000 ways that won't work."

43: Barbados 2

On my first and only visit to the island of Barbados, four other guys and I from St. Augustine stayed in a two-bedroom, one-bath home on the hill overlooking Soup Bowl, which is on the northeast side of the island. The people of Barbados, known locally as Bajan, were exceedingly friendly and helpful until the morning we left when we were robbed of everything except passports, as if to suggest: "We want you to leave. Now." The Bajans were slow-moving in speech and action, the tropical wind setting the cadence for their lives. The only exception to the slow-moving rhythm was the taxi drivers, who scared the hell out of us every time we took a car to Bridgetown, the capital, to party. The taxis, without exception, would exceed the speed limit by double, hugging the mountain roads with two tires in the air. They would pass on curves and play chicken with buses. Were we not liquored up, we would have died from heart failure.

One day at Soup Bowl, the water was as clear as gin and the surface a sheet of glass, and a few of us were catching overhead rights. It was lunchtime and I happened to mention to one of the two locals surfing the break that I was hungry. He immediately dove off his board to the reef, surfacing with a sea urchin. He somehow cracked it open, breaking it in half. He pulled out the grayish meat, saying, "Lunch mon?"

I've wondered about this moment for many years. It's stuck with me because of what the local's hospitality said to me. His act, while practical and a way to solve the minor problem of my hunger, was more than what it was — to me. One surfer to another, and as total strangers, he wanted to help me. I know that such acts are not limited to surfing. And yet, this man's act was wrapped up in the glide. Would he have shown me the same kindness on land? Maybe.

44: Baja

I had a similar experience in Baja, Mexico.

A friend and I were camped three hours from the nearest store and two hours from the nearest paved road. Our tents and truck were close to the water and near some of the few shade trees for miles.

One day, around lunchtime, four Mexican fishermen pulled into "our campsite." Their boat, which was distressed looking, painted white and made from strips of narrow pieces of wood, was 16-to-18 feet long. In the bow of the boat sat an ancient, large compressor, to which they attached a long green garden-like hose. The compressor pumped air into the hose so they could dive for clams the size of a person's palm. The men would take turns diving up to one hundred feet with the hose, taking breaths when needed, gathering clams into a bag from the seafloor. The men were all rugged and brown with thick hands and no shirts or shoes. One of the men had scars across his chest.

All of them were hardened by the sun and ocean. As they beached their boat at our feet, they looked fierce, and I was nervous. The fight or flight chemicals started percolating. My hand went to my side where I had a large knife hanging on my belt.

After they exited their rickety wooden boat, we quickly learned that we were in their daily lunch spot, and the spot where they took their siestas. We made small talk and offered them some of our ridiculously cheap, Pancho Villa Tequila. They refused our liquor and instead offered some of their own Jose Cuervo Gold.

After sharing the bottle and communicating in broken Spanish with them, we got a fire going and cooked fresh fish. We rolled the fish in fresh tortillas that they produced from a cotton sack. One of the men said his wife had made them that morning.

And then the Barbados-like moment happened: One of the Mexicans got a clam out of his diver-bag, and I offered to cook it. He said "No" and then took a large bone-handle knife, opened the clam, and offered it to me raw. I hesitated. The moment felt steeped in adventure. I scooped the massive clam from its shell, the meat still dripping salt water, and ate the clam. The clam was, without a doubt, one of the most tender I had ever put in my mouth. He smiled. There was an immediate connection between us.

The sea had brought us close, if only for a moment and if only as strangers.

Adventures come in many different forms — physical, spiritual, and emotional. They all have their rewards. Adventure adds life to life. Adventure pushes the boundaries of what has been known, expected, and helps to make a person unique. Adventure helps to recreate a person's sense of identity, enlarging the world and a sense of self. Adventure pushes the adventurer to ask, "Who am I?" and "Where is my life heading?" and "What do I want from life?"

The disciples of Jesus must have asked themselves related questions as they walked the dusty roads of ancient Palestine. The four gospels never mention any of the disciples asking these exact questions but surely at night as they fell asleep on a woven mat, their tired bodies, and anxious spirits grateful for the roof over their heads, they must have silently wondered to themselves, "Where is my life heading?" They probably thought Jesus was going to summon a supernatural army to drive the Romans from their homeland, which would leave them in good places to assume some cabinet position in the new administration. And just as surely, they must have asked themselves or one another, "Why am I — why are we – so drawn to this man that we are following him around the countryside and perhaps to our own death?"

I have asked myself comparable questions — not about death — but questions about why I am drawn to Jesus and where my life is heading because of following or trying to follow him. It is never easy to follow in the footsteps of a historical figure who lived before history was written as history. In the case of Jesus (and all other historical figures prior to the Enlightenment,) history was not necessarily communicated in the same manner that we, today, attempt to communicate history. History was not the reporting of fact as we understand fact. History was conceived as detailing a story that may or may not be historically factual but religiously true. This is an important distinction. While I do not believe that every word or story written in the Bible is historically factual, I do believe that it is true, or at least much of it. Truth and fact are dissimilar categories and attempt to answer different questions.

45: Baja 2

One question that regularly surfaces when I'm in a reflective mood, which often happens when I surf alone, is "Why am I a pastor? Why a pastor and not an attorney, fulltime professor of philosophy or religion (I've taught part-time at Flagler College), or a psychologist?" In other words, "Why this life and not some other life?" It's not a complete mystery why we enter certain fields and choose courses of study. On the one hand, we are born with natural gifts. On the other hand, there are the skills we develop through experience. On the third hand, if there were three hands, there is the issue of timing. And, on the fourth hand, there is Divine Providence.

For me, Divine Providence, which is the all-caring attitude of God toward all living beings, answers as many questions as it raises. My experience suggests that Providence is the thread that holds the quilt together. I have always felt the hand of God, even when I did not believe in God. But to become a pastor? How, I marvel, could such a thing take place? Only Providence.

During the month I spent camping in the Baja, I did a lot of contemplating and soul-searching. I was twenty-five and I didn't think much about God, but more about myself and questions of life. I sought something that I would not have called God; I was a self-declared agnostic, which means I didn't think there was enough empirical evidence to make a final judgment about the existence of God. And yet, in even this mood I see the sovereign hand of God moving and guiding me to where I am today.

The camping in Baja was superb. It was a good month. I spent hours upon hours, every day, lounging under small trees. I sat in the shade, half-heartedly fishing, thinking about life, and enjoying the expansive silence. My thoughts over that month were my best company.

I remember how large the night skies were. The fires on the beach would burn and I would eat fresh fish that had been cooked over flames of driftwood. Once, while cooking recently caught fish, I watched two sea snakes. The snakes, which glowed in the dark, swam onto the sand near the fire. They were long with white bellies and very pretty. They twirled together like lovers.

Each night, after dinner, I would recline on the sand and watch the stars that form the Southern Cross. The cross hung in the night sky and symbolized everything, spiritually speaking, that I had cast aside. Any formal association with a religious tradition I put behind me. But there in Baja the cross hung in the southern sky. I stared at it, night in and night out. The cross stared down at me.

One night when I was lying on the sand with a bottle of tequila looking at that giant cross, completely mesmerized by the configuration of the stars, I wondered what had happened to my love of the cross, to my love of the Christ, to my appreciation of religion in general.

There were coyotes who didn't mind coming around the camp. The voices of the coyotes were not new to me; I had heard them in the Big Bend of Texas. Somehow, though, the voices of these coyotes seemed more dangerous in Mexico. I loved their sounds. Their barks made me feel alive. They made me feel wild. The voices of the coyotes stayed with me longer than anything else.

After one month, I left the peninsula and drove to Florida, where my grandmother greeted me at her door and, taking one look at my spindly frame and tired eyes, quickly fixed eggs, grits, and toast. Even during that breakfast, I heard the coyotes. In my mind, I heard them bark and howl even as my grandmother chatted away and refilled my coffee. And now, decades later, I see the hand of Divine Providence weaving its way through my journey—through the Southern Cross and the voices of coyotes.

When we're in the thick of a tough situation or find ourselves in an intellectual or spiritual crisis, it can be hard to sense or find God, even though the hand of Divine Providence is holding us. While surfing and on many occasions in the water waiting for a wave, I've reflected on how God's presence is best seen in hindsight. As I've sat on my longboard, it has seemed to me that Divine Providence is like the ocean that holds me and my board in a great body of love.

46: Faithlessness

After my month in Baja, I spent a week in Florida with family. Hanging out in St. Augustine, I spent a weekend celebrating of a former religion teacher, The Reverend Dr. Mattie Hart, who was retiring. She was the professor who some years before had unknowingly guided me onto the road of skepticism.

I enjoyed the weekend with old college friends from the philosophy and religion department. My plans were to leave on Monday for Jacksonville but was asked by Dr. Hart to visit with her on Tuesday. I gladly accepted the invitation.

We met at Scarlet O' Hara's, a small restaurant and bar in the historic district of St. Augustine. It was a March afternoon. We found our way to the back and sat on stools around a small circular table supported by an aged barrel. I ordered a beer, as did Dr. Hart. After spending time detailing my latest adventures, surfing and otherwise, we began talking about God.

I am always ready to talk about God with people whose faith or intellect I respect, or whose questions are genuine. That is one of the reasons I became a pastor. Certainly, that is one of the reasons why I have always wrestled, like Jacob at the Jabbok River, with religious mystery. Theology (God-talk) was, and is, a very enjoyable way for me to spend an afternoon. Serious God-talk is, at least to me, inspiring. Such conversations may, and often do, open new worlds, and offer deeper perspectives on life. But not all serious God-talk is the same. I would rather talk seriously with a curious two-year-old about God than an adult whose faith knows no questions. Certainties are no substitute for faith. Certainties often curb a poetic imagination that engenders a rich religious life. There can be a dynamic equivalent between certainty and shallow faith. If ever I am made to choose between a theological dogma that precludes mystery or a mystery that precludes dogma, I will always choose mystery. Mystery has sustained me more than certainty.

Dr. Hart and I talked about God and drank beer. It felt holy. There is something sacred about sharing a beer, or a bottle of wine with a friend who knows your struggles, loves, and pain. Moments such as these are even more sacred when the conversation is about the very God who created you, your friend, and the beer or wine that you happen to be consuming. We sat imbibing in the corner of a bar whose walls were washed in the diffused orange light of a late March afternoon. Our conversation turned very personal as I told Dr. Hart of how God was no longer in my life, in any personal sense. I tried my best to sound intelligent and philosophically astute. I tried to impress her with the books I had read and the thoughts I had thought. I tried to show off my years roaming from coast to coast. I tried to impress her with my depth. But she wasn't impressed because my depth was, in part, a charade.

What I was trying to do was keep her distant enough so I wouldn't be faced with any personal responsibility for my lack of belief. This is important: Whether one believes or doesn't believe, intellectual responsibility remains.

Faithlessness has many forms because it has many different foundations. My faithlessness, if indeed it was faithlessness, stemmed from my philosophic objections to the existence of God and the acute desire to be free of a faith that kept me from experiencing the world in all its many forms. For many religious people, faith in God keeps them from being who God created them to be. Fear has a way of binding us with the very thing we love. Fear has a way of masquerading as faith.

Dr. Hart saw through my philosophic objections and my fear. As I sipped my beer she said to me, staring directly into my eyes, "Hunter, I don't get the impression that you are even open to God." It's impossible to say why words work on us the way they do. Words have power. Words create new realities. As the Gospel of St. John says, *"In the beginning was the Word and the Word was with God and the Word was God. He was with God in the beginning."* I did not take the glass from my lips but held it there, the beer lingering on my mouth. Dr. Hart's statement hit me between my eyes. It was a summons to question in a new way. And I had nothing to say in return. Not because she was wrong, but because, for the first time in years, I was confronted with the amazingly simple fact that I wasn't open to God's existence. Dr. Hart was right: God had become an idea, abstract, and unimportant to the living of my life. The possibility of God was interesting to think about, but God's existence was not a real possibility to me. I had ceased to be open to the potentiality of God. But in that instant, as I took a sip of my beer, God became real, again. A real possibility. I was coming full circle. The voice that had originally given rise to my eventual disbelief now gave rise to belief. The beer became like Communion wine.

47: God's Mystery

I am afraid that most people never know the mystery of God. Not even people who profess belief. Indeed, most people, even people who profess belief, seem to relegate God to caverns of unimportance, like some distant planet they know exists but has no gravitational pull on their lives. It's very odd that this creating power of the universe can be pushed to a small, dusty corner of one's life only to be extricated on Christmas, Easter, baptisms, weddings, funerals, or moments of crises. How can this be? How can a presence that defies limits be limited by our needs? For many of us, God is a God of convenience. For many of us, God is a drive-thru God.

48: God's Power

I have always felt the leading hand of God, even when I did not believe in God. During those years of unbelief, I understood that guiding hand as Truth — Plato's ideal. But I now believe, looking backward over many years, that God was at work in my life, even within my unbelief. God is always at work, even within the lives of those who do not believe in God. It never ceases to amaze me that some of my well-meaning sisters and brothers of Christian faith think, live, and speak as if God's Providence can be thwarted by a person's unbelief. As if God's power or existence, by being denied, becomes a moot point. As if a person's denial of God's existence makes God non-existent. As if unbelief can thwart God's purpose and ability to lead and guide the one who does not believe. God's mystery and love are larger than my ability — or anyone's ability — to deny this mystery and love. Despite what some may claim, nothing can impede or hinder God's tenacity and power, presence, and influence. Not removing prayer from schools, or removing the Ten Commandments from public life, or the slow demise of the centrality of the Church in America or Europe. The breakdown of the traditional family or rise of materialism and individualism cannot hinder God's work because God isn't dependent or contingent upon what we believe or do. God is Other. To suggest that God can be stymied by us is silly. God's mystery pervades all that is.

Every time I glide, I experience the mystery of God. I talk to this mystery, mostly silently and in my head. We commune together on the sea. Sometimes I speak aloud, as if the waves are my companions in the divine-human conversation, their presence adding another dimension to the relationship. I question the mystery, love the mystery, agree with the mystery, plead with it, admire it, and stand in awe of this presence as the most beautiful suffusion of life possible.

My experience in life and my experience of God, as well as my reading of the Bible and other texts, have led me to believe that this Creator would not, as some profess, consign people to an eternity of suffering. Can a good parent forever punish — intentionally injure with pain — their child? It makes no theological sense, exactly because it makes no anthropological sense. Would I, even for a moment, ever consider burning my son with a cigarette? Of course not. To suggest that God, who is love incarnate, would do something akin to this is theological madness. To make such a claim and to insist upon the veracity of this claim by lifting a handful of Bible verses, or verses from the Quran says more about the one making the claim than it says about God.

Years ago, as I was leaving Flagler College, where I once taught a course on world religions, I walked past two young men holding inflammatory religious signs and speaking loudly at students. The young men with signs were yelling threats of hell at students. When I tried to speak kindly to one of the young men, he rebuffed me. When I asked if we might speak privately about his method of spreading the love of God, he shouted at me, pointed a finger, and then promptly condemned me to hell.

I guess the young man had not read the latest news. A poll just recently released by the Pew Forum on Religion and Public Life showed that condemning secular humanists to burn in hell for eternity is not an effective means to convert them. The study interviewed over 10,000 participants by phone and found that of 2,342 professed secular humanists who were told they would suffer the fires of hell for their disbelief, not even one converted to believing in God.

Hell should never be wielded like a club by religious folk. Who is going to hell, if indeed anyone is going to hell, and for what, is God's business. It is not my business or your business to condemn or assign people to torment.

The Greek New Testament concept of hell originally referred to a garbage-dump outside of Jerusalem where fire continuously burned trash. The Greek word, *Ghenna*, does not appear very many times in the New Testament. In one text, hell is described as the punishment for calling a sister or brother "fool (Matthew 5:22)" and in another text hell is offered as the punishment for despising "little ones," i.e., "outcasts" (Matthew 18:9).

All of this is to say that any reading of the Bible that focuses on the fear of hell as a means for converting the unchurched or de-churched is a poor tool. But such attempts at converting those who don't believe do a fantastic job of engendering negative stereotypes of Christians. So, if you happen to be the type of Christian who points your finger at people and then beats them over the head with threats of hell, you may want to examine how many fingers are pointing back at yourself. You may also want to recall the words of Jesus in the Sermon on the Mount: "Not everyone who says to me "Lord," "Lord" will enter the Kingdom of Heaven."

49: Sea Creatures

Good waves are about as far as one can get from hell, even when sea creatures among the waves hit the internal panic button of the surfer.

One early summer morning it was clear and hot. The waves were chest high and long. They were well-shaped and fun. As I paddled over to a friend named Beth, she said a manatee had scared her half-to-death when it surfaced next to her board. A moment later, the brown head of the small manatee rose to the surface next to my board, brushing my knee. My heart almost jumped out of my chest as the nostrils breathed out the most rancid air I've ever smelled. The air smelled like rotten eggs and kelp and sewage. Its half-dollar size black eyes looked at me. Its head rested on my board, and it tried to gently put its mouth on my rail, as if it planned to take a bite out of the foam and fiberglass. I scratched its leathery head and gently pushed myself away from its mouth.

The manatee followed me as I paddled south. Stopping to scan the horizon for a set, the manatee brushed my feet as it swam beneath me. The sensation sent chills through me. Anytime a thing bumps the leg of someone surfing, the feeling is fear. Immediately, we think shark! Even the touch of a small jellyfish can trigger an internal reaction hugely disproportional to its size, power, and intent.

Surfers accept that sea creatures are moving around beneath us. We accept that some of these creatures have the capability to inflict harm, even death. But the glide overpowers any fears of the unthinkable. The glide, when the surf is good, is an on-ramp to something close to heaven—and as far from thoughts of hell as I can imagine.

50: Offshore

One fall day, I surfed at sunrise and again in the afternoon. The waves were forecast to be good in the morning with offshore winds, but the wind was not favorable. Around noon I noticed through the window in my study at the church that the wind had gone offshore. I saw the sable palm leaves rattling from west to east. I checked the magnolia tree and it, too, was lightly edging eastward.

By late afternoon I made it to the beach and the wind was due west at 10 knots. Perfect. The ground swell was pumping. The tide had just turned from low to high. Few people were out. Just a couple of guys south of me at the pier. Not a soul out at my break, FA. The shore break was pounding hard. I waded out, pushed my board through the first couple of waves but then read the third wave wrongly and got slammed, the board being ripped from my hands, my left hand hurting from the force of the wave.

I paddled to the lineup. The waves were coming in sets of two. The buoys said the swell was at 13 seconds from a large storm system in the mid-Atlantic. The sun was bright, and the wind pushed against the faces of the waves, spray coming off the backside. The overhead peaks were rolling in, slow moving hills of energy, soft and pretty, thick, and well groomed. The peaks and lines with soft shoulders are my favorite type of wave to ride: lots of turns with a tender power that propels the glide with a grace that is harder to uncover when the waves are breaking hard, top to bottom. Surfing on these waves makes it possible to take one's time to make cutbacks and turns. There's more time for thought, which allows for a more artistic approach to the canvass of a wave.

The swell was deeply therapeutic, which I much needed after the recent presidential election. It's so strange how we let ourselves get caught up in national drama we have no control over. We whine and fuss, cuss, and spit, feeling anxious over spectacles beyond our power to change. And then, as I waited for a wave, I remembered the Serenity Prayer: "Lord, grant me the serenity to accept the things I cannot change, courage to change the things I can, and wisdom to know the difference." There is peace in the acceptance of reality, what is real, what is really happening, what is. That is not to say that we should not work for the change we envision in our family, ourselves, our community, or our world. If we desire to become a better surfer, we should push ourselves to become a better surfer. But acceptance of the present circumstance as we work for a different future has the power to penetrate our heart with peace. Contentment breeds tranquility. Apathy breeds bitterness. And therein is the difference between a positive, hope-filled acceptance of the present and a resignation to bitterness.

I caught a wave and slid tenderly onto a small, delicate face, dipping the fingertips of my right hand into the water as I moved rapidly down the line, and the chest-high lip pitched outward. The golden rays of the sun pierced the fragile movement of the wave. The pitching lip almost seemed reluctant to break, as if it didn't want to expend or expel the energy that had brought it to this point in its life. I watched the lip, and I rode down the line, walking to the nose of my board, my left toes hung over the tip of the board, for just a second, and I felt like I was walking on water. It's as close to divinity as I will ever come.

51: Faith

God, I believe, wants us to be happy, but personal happiness is not the goal and end of life. Nevertheless, I believe God wants us to engage in activities that fill us with gratitude and joy. God, I believe, wants me to surf.

There is a small but thorny issue with my belief. Namely, anytime anyone makes a claim about God, the claim is faith-based. And any claim about God must be a tentative claim. A claim about God must, by its very nature, be a tentative claim because God is beyond any claim, we might make about God. God is beyond our "yes's" and our "no's," our "this's" and our "that's." God is beyond our faith-suppositions, assumptions of intuition, and our philosophical theories. God is beyond our convictions of truth and our opinionated principles. God is beyond our understanding and our categories. That is why God is God and we are not God. So, when I say, "God, I believe, wants us to engage in activities that fill us with gratitude and joy," this claim of mine cannot be substantiated by me. Conversely, neither can my claim be proven false. Like truth claims big and small, my "I believe" statement is a faith statement. God wants me to practice the glide.

My "I believe" statement is a faith statement, so it's not a statement of certainty. Faith and doubt are kissing cousins. But faith and certainty exist in a relationship much like oil and water. Faith and certainty are apples and oranges. Faith and certainty are working from two entirely different paradigms of reality. And that is why religion and spirituality are called "faith" and not a certainty. But religion is not alone in its faith claims. Fields of science are also based in a faith that cannot be unequivocally proven or disproven. Even atheism is faith-based, much to the chagrin of atheists.

Like so many things in life, surfing requires faith. I have faith in my ability to execute the glide that helps me take the first paddle stroke that guides me into the lineup. Someone might argue that is my experience, proven over many years like a hypothesis, tested and true, that gives me the confidence to paddle out. This is true — now. But not at first. First, it is a leap of faith. To catch the first wave takes a certain confidence in one's potential ability to catch a wave. Faith in what might be. Faith sees beyond what is readily knowable or experienced. But even now, I have faith that I will perform the glide without getting eaten by a hammerhead. I have faith that I will not bump my head on the board when wiping out, knocking myself unconscious in the water. I have faith that I won't get held down by a wave and run out of air. Life is comprised of one faith judgment after another. We live, breathe, and move based on faith.

52: Hold Down

One of the worst hold downs in my life happened at Hermosa beach, Costa Rica. It was 1989 and I was there for the summer with several other guys from Flagler College. Back then, Costa Rica had not yet become a haven for ex-pats, eco-tourism, surf trips, drugs, and prostitution. San Jose, its capital, was full of horns and diesel and too many people. But places like Jaco Beach and Hermosa Beach, both which are in Puntarenas on the Central Pacific coast, were Spartan places with dirt roads and barely a restaurant. They were places brimming with hospitality and quietude. And they were very inexpensive. There were not even surf shops in these places. No hard drugs or gang-related issues. Just Third World beach towns that moved at the pace of a snail.

In 1989, there was virtually nothing in Hermosa Beach. A cow pasture and large Guanacaste tree were the markers for surfers looking for the surfing spot in Hermosa Beach. The tree had gangly roots and a large canopy, with thick branches waving in all directions. The tree was in the middle of nowhere. Just off a two-lane highway, we encountered carts pulled by steers or oxen. The jungle crept into the dirt road, which was full of potholes and animal dung. Mountains bordered one side of the road.

The color of the sand at Hermosa Beach ranges from mahogany brown to black. It glistens in the sun and gets exceptionally hot on the feet. It is filled with volcanic minerals and lava fragments. It's fair to say that the wave also can be volcanic.

Early one morning, I stood on the black sand watching a few guys in the water. The waves were double-overhead and spread apart. I made it to the lineup. Glassy conditions. Beautiful. Perfect. I paddled into my first wave, which was a left. It was a thick and meaty turquoise cliff, hollow and powerful. I didn't make the wave and was not ready for the hold-down. I hit the water hard. All the air left my lungs, like I was I hit in the stomach by a hard punch. I could feel the wave turn and twist me as I was shaken like a ragdoll. Pinned hard, I thought, "I'm going to drown. I have no air. I cannot get up." A moment later fire-colored stars danced before my eyes, my lungs were burning, and an involuntary reflex began forcing me to take a breath of water. My lips parted to suck in the sea. My head pounded and adrenaline coursed through my body. It was a moment of realization: I was free from everything except survival. At the last imaginable moment, I surfaced, gasping air. I paddled in, sat under the large tree, and watched my friends. The near-drowning was an encounter, of sorts, with freedom—the kind of freedom that exists when life is balanced with what feels like near death. The experience of being held underwater until I thought my head and lungs would burst from lack of oxygen became for me a metaphor for a greater understanding of spiritual freedom. It is a freedom that comes from within and is not easily found, but often discovered through struggle and grace. It is often through struggle that we come to see new horizons within ourselves.

53: Synch

I once solo-paddled the New River in a 16-foot green canoe from West Jefferson, North Carolina, which is close to the headwaters of the river, to West Virginia, taking out at Bluestone Dam. It was 211 miles – many thousands of paddle strokes – during twelve cold, blustery November days, many of which were laced with struggle. Each time my paddle stroked the dark river, there was also a stroke of freedom, a simultaneous journey inward and outward. In some sense, whether we know it or not, each of us is always on an outward and inner journey. We are all paddling a river, so to speak.

My experience suggests that we are all hunting for the synchronicity that Carl Jung wrote of — the best life, whose confluence comes from dovetailing the outer and inner life. I believe to experience this reality; a touch of Providence is needed. When the outward journey mirrors the inward journey, and vice-versa, we experience what Jung's student, Joseph Campbell, termed "bliss." A completeness. This completeness is what I experience when I am surfing and my toes edge over the nose of the board, or I hear the soft thunder of a barrel, or I make a fluid turn that feels like embodied grace. Synchronicity.

Sometimes the synchronicity that we seek evades us. Like when I surf and I don't feel coordinated. It happens more often then I care to admit.

I recall this one time in the fall when the water had turned cooler, and the surface of the ocean was choppy from a northeast wind. The wind with its slight chill started irritating me. I began to take the annoying gusts of wind personally. The seawater, at 70 degrees, with the sea breeze, made me shiver. I tried to have fun, to enjoy the glides, to appreciate the wait, to admire the sky, to regard the pelicans with esteem, but to no avail. The outer and inner experience would not mesh. There was no synchronicity. Even the sun, in its fall softness, could not lift my spirits. My arms and legs felt sluggish and heavy.

Prior to paddling out, I thought that 30 minutes of Yin-style yoga and the quick bike to the beach would enliven my body and mind and I would find a few good glides, despite the chop and wind and cold. But I was wrong.

The waves were soft and mushy, chest high, the form fair at best.

My first two waves were lefts, and I fell on the second wave like some kid who had just begun learning how to surf. My frustration grew. My mind kept turning over a situation happening at the church, which is not particularly common for me. Typically, when I am surfing, I am surfing. I can leave the land behind and all that the land signifies. But not this day. My mind was cluttered. I was far from being focused and my surfing showed it. I did not feel an inner tranquility.

The fall from the second wave pinched something in my left knee and it began to ache. I took a third wave, a right, and it closed out—but before I could pop over the back of the lip, my board got hung up, knocked to the side and I fell, again.

Somedays, it seems the best we can do is just go through the motions. Somedays, we must put one foot in front of the other, keep our heads down and keep trying. And even when we keep trying, somedays a good glide is not to be. That is the nature of surfing — and life. Yet, even when synchronicity is absent from our work or play, even then meaning and Providence snake their way through difficult days. It's on these kinds of days that we must surrender. Wave the white flag. Acknowledge the good attempt and admit the failure, or however we choose to qualify our inability to glide or live exactly how we want to glide or live. Often, when we surrender, it's at this moment that we gain perspective, and our mind and body begin to align. And if we can laugh at ourselves and how seriously we are taking the glide, or life, that may take us even a step farther on the path of integration.

54: Ebb and Flow

You have good days, and you have bad days. Days when everything comes together and you're dancing on clouds. Then there are days when you can barely put your shorts on the right way. Life moves up and down, a fluid ebb and flow. The tide always changes. So why, I often wonder, can't I just be patient? Nothing is permanent in this life except change and the love of God. These things combined, more than anything else, give me a sense of inner freedom. There is great comfort to be found in the fact that everything changes, everything passes and through it all, God is love. There is great well- being to be found in patience.

Sometime before 1200 the word patience came into Old English, being borrowed from Old French, being borrowed from the Latin word *patiencia*. In all three languages the word patience means to calmly endure.

Patience, the ability to calmly endure, is not something many of us are born with—myself included. Few of us can wait for anything – even waves — without anxiety, though practicing the glide does strengthen patience. Surfing has taught me that patience is an attribute that most often comes with experience, but not always with age. More accurately, as Saint Augustine put it, "Patience is the companion of wisdom." That is, patience is a learned practice. It's my experience that patience is closer to art than science. Patience is more like dance and less like structural engineering.

In the summer I cultivate the art of patience more readily. To me, summer has a different rhythm than the rest of the year. Summer seems to saunter through the day, stopping to smell a flower or swing in a hammock. During summers, I am most able to do as Ralph Waldo Emerson wrote, "Adopt the pace of nature, whose secret is patience."

It's no secret that many of us have too little patience. Patience is not a virtue that's readily cultivated by 21st century Americans. We are, after all, people who live hurried, anxious lives — but not necessarily lives of quality. I continue to learn how crucial patience is to a well-lived life. It's my judgment that a well-lived life possesses the quality of being present in the moment rather than living for the future. To accomplish this goal, a person must practice patience.

Two places where I regularly show the greatest lack of patience are traffic jams and grocery store checkout lines. These situations have this in common: both force me to pause in my execution of a goal. Both situations stall forward momentum. Both situations have the propensity to let the lion of anxiety out of the cage. Both situations test my strength to calmly endure.

It's not that I am an impatient person. In fact, I have been told— albeit by few people — that I am a very patient person. I am usually the last one to roll my eyes at the person in the express line with thirty items when the sign clearly states twenty items or less. Patience, like all virtues, does not come naturally. In this way, I suppose virtue is like most things: practice makes proficient.

On some days, even while surfing, patience eludes me. When the waves are bad, I can find myself being impatient as I look for a good wave. And when the waves are good, I can find myself hurrying to catch as many good waves as possible. Relaxation and pure enjoyment are banished in favor of expediency. And that, I suppose, is part of being human — and only human. It's easy to forge that nothing temporal endures: no situation, no swell, no matter how bad or good, will continue ad infinitum. Nothing lasts, except God. And that is exactly how God created the nature and fabric of the cosmos. Everything runs its course — your life, my life, the sun, your favorite pet, your favorite break. And if God created life to be impermanent, then it must, ultimately speaking, be good. Or, at least, that is what I tell myself on days when I'm aggravated, or days past when I knew acute physical pain and psychological despair. I tell myself: This too shall pass.

55: A Good Wave

I watch as a wave moves in my general direction. It bowls up in an unexpected manner, the sides of the wave pushing the middle into an A-frame slab that looks exceedingly fun. In the moment, I forget the former wipeouts, the throbbing knee, the frustrations of the day and focus upon the fun peak that is about to be mine. I paddle hard, catch the wave, and slide into a sweet waist-high line that is fast with a strong wall that is not closing out. I glide faster and faster, dancing forward on the board. Arms raised over my head, I near the nose and arch my back to counterbalance and maintain my position on the board and the wave. I back step, crouch low and speed to the beach, stepping off my board as the fin begins to drag in the sand. A good wave. Finally, on this day, a much-needed good wave. It's true, yet again: A frustrating day is immediately transformed into a good day. Change is the only constant, and patience to wait for change is, at times, the only power we possess over a situation.

56: Wetsuits

Seasons change, even in Florida. Sometimes people get the impression that all of Florida is of one climate and disposition. Nothing could be further from the truth. In Northeast Florida, we have the changes that go from real hot, hot, warm, cool, and cold. The cold is not usually long or permanent in the winter months but comes in fits and spurts and lasts for a week or two, then abates, then comes again. Mostly, however, we stay in flip-flops. But the ocean temperature begins to cool down by late October, so a vest is needed. By November, a spring suit is needed, then late November through the following March, a full suit. These patterns for wetsuits reflect the Florida native and not the recent northern transplant.

I have never liked chilly water. Or even cool water, by which I mean water below 75 degrees. I like my ocean water warm to hot. I hate wetsuits.

I don't like putting them on or taking them off. I don't like surfing in wetsuits, but neither do I like cold water. So, every year for 37 years I have donned the rubber that keeps out the cold. The rubber neoprene wraps my body, constricting movement, making it more difficult to paddle but allowing surfing in the winter. I honestly don't know how people surfed cold water before wetsuits. But they did. And I suppose, if push came to shove, I would do the same.

A long time ago I came to grips with a simple and unavoidable fact: If I wanted to surf year-round, then I must wear a wetsuit. And that is part of life: compromise, being flexible. I may not want to wear a wetsuit, but I do want to surf. I may not want to do something, but if by doing it I am rewarded, then the scales tip the balance in favor of doing it — wearing the wetsuit. In surfing and in life, the art of compromise with others and oneself is as necessary as air to breathe or water to drink. Without compromise, life becomes brittle and relationships to self or others are fractured. To paraphrase the Tao Te Ching, the principal text of Taoism, "One must be strong enough to bend." So, I bend, twist, pull, and push until the neoprene suit covers my body, allowing me to paddle out and revel in glassy winter waves, which always helps me become a better man, better husband, and

better father, or so my wife continually tells me.

As I wait for another wave on this chilly but sunny day, I watch a shrimp boat a couple of miles offshore. The crew must be hauling in their nets, because there is a gray cloud hovering over and trailing behind the boat. The cloud – a flock of birds – gulls, terns, and other small fish eaters moves quickly.

From this distance, the cloud reminds me of a dust storm I once saw in the desert of Syria, close to Palmyra. We had just finished viewing the ruins where Queen Zenobia had dared to stand against the Roman Empire 2,000 years before. The battle was quick and decisive, and the queen was no longer a queen. As we stood next to our travel van, off in the distance we could see a horizon that was gray and moving toward us. Our guide started yelling in Arabic, "Yellah, Yellah!" which means "Hurry, Hurry!" The dust storm was unlike anything I had ever seen — or have seen since that day. I was transfixed as it moved rapidly toward us swallowing the horizon in dust.

The gray cloud of seabirds moving around the shrimp boat remind of that day in Syria. The birds swarm and move as if they had choreographed the scene before acting it out. It looks like a mid-air dance.

I look toward the beach and see another surfer standing with his board. It's an acquaintance of mine that I see on a regular basis. We surf together but we do not see each other outside of the water. Truth be told, I do not want to hang out with him because he is very "I" centered. He's nice enough, but there has never been an occasion while surfing with him or checking the waves from the beach with him that he has once asked me anything about myself. It is always and only about what he has been doing or where he is going. I watch as he pulls his board from the saddle on his bicycle. His bike, like mine, leans against a dune with small sea oats waving in the breeze. As he walks to the water's edge, I catch a tiny peeler and go skimming across the top, my smile wide and full.

57: Solo Sessions

Surfing makes me happy. But surfing is not the only physical activity that makes me smile. Through the years I have smiled playing tennis, golf, mountain biking, fishing, hiking, snorkeling, snow skiing, water skiing, sailing, canoeing, rock climbing, mountain climbing, hunting, and birdwatching. I have found happiness in hard manual labor and slow strolls on the beach with my wife. I have found happiness sitting by a fire in the woods. I have found happiness in prayer and meditation and in making love. I have found happiness sitting quietly in the winter or summer sun, as well as drinking rum with a friend, or, a long time ago, doing drugs. But surfing is, for me, the greatest stoke. The glide produces a mysterious giddiness that defies understanding. Why does moving upon the surface of the ocean give rise to such happiness? What is it about the activity of surfing that produces a feeling of elation?

It was almost dusk. The wind was light offshore. The waves were stomach high, and the sun was slowly melting into the western sky. The sand dunes and sea oats, because of their relative height from my place in the water, concealed the bottom third of the sinking sun. The clouds were pink, like cotton candy with a milky orange lining. No one else was in the water or on the beach and I was stunned at my good fortune. It was quiet. An osprey flew overhead with a large mullet flapping in its talons. I paddled for a beautiful peak and took off right. I took a high line then quickly went toward the trough, made a fine bottom turn, and came up under the falling lip which grazed my head. The wave was fully lit by soft rays from the melting sun, and I made a graceful cutback on the shoulder, dropping my back knee, spraying the backside of the wave. I cut back right and continued to glide, making it through a middle section that was thick and fast, but regained momentum on the inside when the wave doubled up and pitched out. I crouched low, putting my right arm into the face of the wave, which slowed my speed enough to get a small tube. And I smiled. But why? Why would such an act produce happiness?

58: Secret Spot

Today was a good day, a joyful day, a day that consisted of me riding my bike two ½ miles into Anastasia State Park to surf the so-called Secret Spot, which is not very secret. The ride was, as always, breathtaking — if not for its dramatic beauty, at least for its total lack of anything constructed by human hands. Sand dunes sit one hundred feet back from the high-tide line and the dunes range from eight to fifteen feet tall, all the dunes forming a continuous sandy wall that separates the ocean from a portion of water called Salt Run. At one time, before the Army Corp of Engineers got ahold of the area, this part of the island was a separate landmass called Conch Island. Today, sea oats dot the sand dunes, their spindly and wiry roots winding down the sugary slopes. Sea turtles of various species make their nests around here, as do migratory birds such as Foster's Tern. There are blankets of Brown-eyed Susan's covering portions of the dunes, their yellow flowers popping with color against the bleached sand.

On the far side of the dunes is Salt Run, which is like a large lagoon that runs for one mile to the Intracoastal Waterway, and into the inlet. It's bordered on the south side by Anastasia State Park and on the north,

Porpoise Point. Near the water of Salt Run there are small mangroves, rattlesnakes, sand spurs the size of baseballs, odd cedar trees and ground cover aplenty. The area is dry and looks full of snakes. Today, I don't stop to climb one of the dunes, but if I did, I would see St. Augustine to the immediate west. I would see the lighthouse, which looms over my son's former elementary school. Today, I bike to what is known as the Secret Spot, pushing through a light west wind and moderately firm sand as the tide draws farther out.

I see no other bicycle tracks, only a few footprints, and I doubt walkers have come this far with boards. The Secret Spot can get good — but not good enough to compel most surfers to walk several miles to get the waves. As I near the spot, I'm surprised to see two bicycles leaning against the large dune. I look to the ocean in time to see a guy catch a beautiful overhead left. I watch as he rides the wave all the way through to the inside, the beach break grinding out spitting barrels. It immediately calls to mind an emasculated Hermosa Beach, Costa Rica.

I peddle just past the parked bikes and rest my own bike against a dune. Although it strikes me as an odd precaution, I put a lock through the tire and frame. Then, I grab my board from the side saddle and pull-out a bar of pinkish wax from the black milk crate that's attached to the rear of the surf rack. I wax my board, then drag a wax comb through the thickening buildup of wax on the board's deck. I paddle out, getting hit by a set, take a small pounding, get back on my board and pull for the horizon.

59: Middle East

Something about the light coming off the high, white dunes brings a sharp memory to mind, which has nothing to do with surfing but was consequential to my journey. In the summer of 2000, I had the fortune of traveling to the Middle East. I spent three-and-a-half weeks engaged in a seminar paid for entirely by a private foundation and a supplement of the Presbyterian Church (USA).

I traveled with twenty-five seminarians from various Protestant traditions and a handful of lay people. Each of us tipped our hats to Providence because we had been handpicked. We were chosen to explore the religious, historical, and political contexts of the six countries we would visit.

I remember many things about my time in the Middle East. I remember five-star hotels and non-stop lectures, the great spiritual sense of every country we experienced, the beautiful and guttural language of Arabic and bottled water. More than anything, though, I remember the wind. Every day a breeze pushed over the sandy ground we walked. The wind blew dust, dirt, images, and thoughts. It blew questions and experiences.

The wind blew the ancient to mind and shuffled my opinions and musing of the present. Every day the wind blew. It carried songs of birds and languid, harmonic music. The wind carried the voices of those long since dead and those yet unborn. The wind carried smells of flowers, spices, and tobacco.

Questions were on the wind. In Baalbek, Lebanon the wind asked: "How, if at all, is my faith, the Christian faith, different than the faith of those who worshiped Jupiter? How, if at all, is the Christian faith any more accurate than ancient Roman religious faith?"

The wind blew in Bosra, Syria and asked: "How, if at all, is the Judeo-Christian understanding of God more expressive of the divine mystery than the Roman Pantheon? How much is faith tied to cultural context and social imagination?"

The wind spoke these questions as I traveled the dusty regions of the Middle East. I continually felt an abiding sense of the ancient humanity that occupied the ruins we traversed. Walking on these ruins with the wind blowing, I felt a connection to those who went before me—a connection to their ruins. The breeze that wrapped my body in Petra, Jordan, wrapped the bodies of the Nabataeans and their civilization 2,000 years ago. The breeze connected me to the past. I was awestruck, not only by the artistic and engineering capabilities of all the ancient people, but also by our common humanity, which felt like a shared breeze on our faces.

For me, this was the most overpowering and staggering element of my trip: the sheer volume of history. History is like quicksand, or like standing in front of the ocean. History is wide beyond comprehension. After traveling through antiquity's mausoleums, I now understand religion and politics (and indeed life itself) through this lens, the lens of history, of context, of cultural imaginations and their interactions with the forces, ideas, and gods (and God), that surrounded their daily lives.

The wind blew. And it blew. The wind blew open the door of history, the expanding horizon in time.

The most acute way I experienced this expanding horizon of time was on the back of a camel climbing the famous Jebel Musa, the Mountain of Moses, in Mount Sinai, Egypt.

The experience was surreal. We woke at 1 a.m., boarded a bus and drove to St. Catherine's Monastery in the Sinai Peninsula of Egypt. It is oldest Christian Monastery in the world. Moonlight bathed the desert floor with an eerie luminescence. We heard soft voices and saw cigarettes burning. The camels were sleeping, along with many of the owners, most of whom were young men and boys.

We hired two dozen camels. Someone grabbed me and motioned for me to climb onto the back of a sleeping giant. The saddle was uncomfortable, and I felt scared. The camel, at the owner's command, rose quickly. And then we were off, me riding and the owner running behind. It was 2 a.m.., and I was riding a camel up Mount Sinai! The expanding horizon of time stretched forth. The camel's name was "Whiskey," which is ironic because Muslims don't drink alcohol. It was as if with each "swoosh" of Whiskey's feet I was being carried not upward to the summit of some mythical highland but inward into the eye of antiquity — the very eyes of Moses. It was the ride up the mountain with the billions of stars and constellations swirling above as the quiet young Bedouin man with an orange ember in his mouth motivated my camel to climb. Yes, it was there that I fell waist-deep into the river of history. There, with a Muslim as my guide.

A strange and haunting wind blew on Sinai.

The young Bedouin man asked me in very broken English to find him work in America. He asked me to send for him. He wrote down his address in Arabic on my notebook. I could not read it. He said, "America number one…"

Yes, the wind blew on Sinai, and it spoke a mouthful. The wind on Sinai spoke many different tongues, many different languages, and carried many different questions.

The wind blew in Jerusalem, that ancient, embattled city of dreams.

The wind in Jerusalem, like all of Israel (or should I say Palestine?), is jumbled rhetoric. So many different nuances to this land. I was astounded to see and feel and hear the webs of religious and political complexities playing themselves out like some nasty childhood block fight. The battle between the Israelis and the Palestinians, between Muslims, Christians, and Jews, the arguments, and lawsuits between various Christian traditions over a particular place. On and on it went.

Then, of course, there is the major and very real threat of war. War between Israel and Syria, or Israel and any Muslim country in the Middle East. Never did my studies, never did my preparatory reading (and there was a lot), brace me for the reality of the situation. The Middle East, including Israel, especially Israel, is a boiling stew of anger, injustice, zealotry, and war.

The wind in the Middle East is complex.

It has an edge to it that at times made me nervous — but less nervous than the night streets of Atlanta or Jacksonville. Of course, the streets of Atlanta or Jacksonville don't carry with them the imminent threat of religious zealots with car bombs — not yet anyhow. The reality of my relative safety as a middle-class white man living in America caused me some amount of discomfort. The hand of Providence seems unfair and even cruel. I have no more right to safety than anyone else, and yet I have more safety than most in the Middle East.

60: Humanity's Pain

As I sit in the ocean and turn my sight to the horizon waiting for a wave, I reflect on the sense of my own humanity and the overall depth of humanity's pain. I saw pain in the Middle East.

But, of course, pain is a stranger to no land. When out of context and traveling, one has a keener eye to pain — especially pain that is atypical or anomalous in one's own context.

While walking through the bazaar in Damascus, Syria, from out of nowhere, a short man hobbled up to me and held out his dirty palm. I looked at him and he smiled a toothless grin. I smiled back. He spoke. "Leprosy." He pointed to his foot, which was black like tar. His ankle was the size of a grapefruit, and his calf had a gaping, black hole. I was stunned and disgusted. He wanted money. For what, I don't know. And I turned away. It was one of the first times in my life that I refused someone in obvious pain. His pain was too horrible for me. I felt ashamed for not dropping a coin into his hand.

It would've cost me so little.

Behind the pain of the Middle East, however, lies lavish hospitality and considerable beauty. The wind carried the pain, hospitality, and beauty together and at times it was impossible to disentangle them.

And then there was the wind of Galilee.

The wind that washed across the face of Jesus. The wind that swept Jesus into the chaos of a similar, if different, entanglement. To know that Jesus walked and ate, healed, and taught with this Galilean wind blowing through his hair just as the wind blew through mine, well, this was overwhelming for me.

It's difficult to describe the power that the imagination of such a place possesses. To see the land where Jesus lived and where his parables originated, put flesh and bone on the Jesus who I've read about since boyhood. Indeed, the entire biblical text took on new proportions in Galilee. The Bible came alive, it became 3-D: the mountains and trees and lake were full of realness. In Galilee, the sayings of Jesus became even more dangerous because they were infused with physicality, even while they remained totally other.

The wind blew us to Greece. And, again, the wind raised questions.

In Corinth, as I sat under a temple dedicated to Apollo, the wind whispered; "What is the difference between worshiping idols and worshiping dogma? What is the difference between ancient idolatry and modern consumerism?" As the wind blew in Corinth, small white clouds floated over the mountains. They reminded me of small theologies and how, in the sea of history, all ideas, concepts, temples, peoples, and empires float over the mountain. All things decay and crumble and are left, inevitably, in ruins, not unlike the great buildings of ancient Greece.

The wind blew. And it blew. And the wind didn't care about theology or politics or anything that vainly attempts to catch it or employ it for gain.

Funny how the light on a sand dune while surfing St. Augustine Beach can call to mind experiences in the Middle East, experiences and thoughts that happened 6,500 miles away and had nothing to do with surfing.

61: Porpoises

Sitting in the lineup, I soon have uninvited but welcome guests. Porpoises appear, the color of an unpolished silver knife blade. The sky is as clear as it will ever be, this day or 1,000 years from now.

The sun is electric yellow. The porpoises, as they roll, are slick in their grayness, shiny in the sun. They are close to me, just a few yards away. I repeatedly tap my hand on the surface of the water in hopes that they will come closer to my position. They don't.

There is always something oddly comforting about the presence of these mammals. It might be as simple as gratitude for a porpoise being a porpoise and not a shark. But it goes deeper than that. It might be the way the porpoises look at me as they breech and roll and play. Or maybe it is the way they play — jumping high and clearing their full body and weight from the ocean, their mouths slightly agape showing small white teeth set in a genuine smile. The appearance of this smile suggests to me that porpoises create fun; they understand play. And their play is resonant with the glide. Yes, they have their own glide. I have seen it. I know this to be true because I have shared many waves with porpoises. They come from nowhere, slightly beneath the surface, riding the face of the wave just in front of or outside of my board. Dolphins know the glide and that is why they smile.

62: A Gift from God

During Hurricane Sandy, when the waves were epic, I was surfing with my friend Joe. It was mid-afternoon on a Sunday and the waves were double-overhead and as good as they ever get in Florida. Offshore wind. Warm water. Sunny.

I was waiting for a wave. I looked to the beach to gauge my position and I saw a young dolphin swimming fast and close by an adult dolphin. And then they caught a beautiful wave. The wave was a right, and the adult headed straight down the face at a sweet angle, the small porpoise following suit.

As I watched them, and as they neared the impact zone, both porpoises, as if on cue, launched themselves from the lip of the wave. As the wave broke both the adult and young porpoise were airborne, many feet above the wave. The west wind was blowing hard, and the spray came off the back of the wave in sheets. Amid this sheet of spray were the soaring silver bodies of the dolphins six feet above the lip. They jumped and flew in tandem, the afternoon light illuminating their nakedness, bright and alive.

It was a moment of sheer exquisiteness. A gift from the sea. A gift from God.

Moments like this have convinced me that surfing is more than the glide. In part, the glide is the wait. It is the ocean. It is the wind. It is the sandbar or reef. It is the energy of the wave. It is a brown pelican dropping heavy from a leaden sky intent upon a mullet. It is the sun and the rain, solitude, and friendship.

Surfing is diverse and numinous because it operates outside the world of economy, utility, and necessity. The glide operates in a world where land rules do not apply, and where the very foundation of creation came into being. In a word, the glide operates in a mystical shadow where life brims with untamed vigor and unexpected dynamism.

This mystical shadow can happen at any moment while surfing. As I watch brown pelicans, they remind me of logs falling from the sky hunting for fast-moving prey. I watch as pelicans circle, gliding on the wind, and then plummet straight down as if they have suddenly died in mid-flight. Down, down, down they go, bringing their full weight and force upon the unknowing baitfish, a splash of water rising three feet in the air. There are also times when the pelicans fly just above the gray sea that looks like steel under a balmy haze of an early warm morning. As they fly inches above the surface, wings spread wide, they glide fast and stealth-like, eyes trained forward as they tilt a wing to compensate for the air being pushed up or out by a passing wave. They are masters of the glide. I have even begun imitating their glide when riding certain waves. I will extend my arms wide as if I am flying, tilting my arm up or down to help maneuver down the line. At times, I am riding a wave as they pass me by, and we glide together, me feeling coordinated with their wisdom. Other times, I watch the pelicans as they fly south or north, a large "V" shape moving through the air like a massive spear point. They do this together, which is a good metaphor for human community: a tribe of like-minded people surrounding us as we make our way through life.

63: Surfing is Individual

I find this kind of camaraderie in my church and local community. I saw this camaraderie play out in the wake of Hurricane Matthew. People's homes were destroyed or damaged beyond being habitable.

I witnessed people reaching out, lending a hand, giving money and time and expertise to assist the needy among us. Surfers were among the victims and Good Samaritans.

Sebastian Junger, the author of *The Perfect Storm*, among other books, published a small work entitled, Tribe. It is a worthy book for people unaccustomed to reflecting on the nature and importance of community. While it is not groundbreaking, it does offer a needed corrective for one of the ailments of modern life: fierce uniqueness. The importance of community is as old as religion itself — whether the religious tradition is Christianity, Judaism, Islam, Hinduism, or Buddhism. People have always known, instinctually, that people need people. And yet we forget —or, more accurately, we subordinate the community to the pathos of individualism — until we are diagnosed with a terminal illness, or we find ourselves alone, broke, ravaged by a hurricane, or without work. We are not islands. We forget that community brings out the best, and the worst, in us. Regardless, like the pelicans flying in the "V" formation to conserve energy and assist the flock, we need each other.

Surfing, however, is not a communal activity, though it may be practiced in community. Surfing is an individual pursuit and a solitary expression and thus, to some philosophical degree, it is anti-communal. No surfer needs another surfer to surf (but we do need shapers) — except the tow-in crowd (That's when a surfer is towed into a breaking wave by a partner driving a personal watercraft, such as a Jet Ski).

The glide, and the necessity to wait to glide, is a deeply personal, albeit not always private endeavor. The glide is not a team sport. And while community may be a part of the glide experience, community is not necessary to the glide. But to communicate the experience of the glide there must be another surfer to share it with. As the saying goes, "Only a surfer knows the feeling."

A surfer can talk about surfing with a non-surfer, but the glide can't be understood by one who has not felt the glide. While the glide doesn't require a community of gliders, conveyance of the art, in any meaningful way, does require community — a tribe. We all need community if only to fully express our inner world of experience.

64: Hurricane

Today, I surfed thigh-to-waist high waves with a hard offshore wind. When the waves broke, the water blew so hard off the back of the lip that it felt like a firehose was being aimed at me.

The beads of water were more like a spray of shot pellets. The mist from the spray looked like it might be carried halfway across the Atlantic Ocean. The wind held me at the top of the small waves, doing its best to keep me from dropping-in, allowing me only to slide onto the face at the last possible second.

The hard offshore wind reminded me of Hurricane Matthew, which, on October 7, 2016, passed thirty miles from the coast of St. Augustine Beach. My journal entry:

"Yesterday, I helped a partially drunken man board up my three east-facing windows. He arrived on time, in blue jeans, and a white T-shirt. Black baseball cap turned backwards. Brown works boots stained with drops of paint and mud. He was a thick man, no more than 5' 8" but weighing 220 lbs. Strong looking and a face of whiskers. About 30 years old.

"He stepped from his red Ford pickup as the oak trees bent and squeaked, leaves flying from their branches like tiny magic carpets, green and brown, headed to God knows where. He grabbed his circular saw from the back seat, walked around to the rear of the truck and dropped the tailgate. He reached for a small Coleman cooler with a white top and red bottom. There were three empty cans of Bud littering the bed of his truck. "Beer?" he asked. "Sure," I said. We cracked our beers and I asked him if he had already had a few. "Just a couple," he said. He reached into his baggy front pockets and pulled out two fingers of whiskey. "Care for one?" He asked, beginning to drag a ladder from the bed. "No, I think I'll pass. I have a lot to do before the evacuation." My response ruined his joy. His face soured and he remarked, "Well grab this plywood and let's get cutting."

Twenty minutes later he was twelve feet up on a ladder as he held, with one hand, half a sheet of plywood. In his other hand he held a drill with a concrete bit that would penetrate our brick. The wind was blowing harder. I wondered if this whole enterprise of boarding up windows was futile. The National Hurricane Center has forecast a storm surge of 9'-11'. Our house sits at 9' above sea level and we live three blocks from the beach.

Winds are forecast at 120 MPH and the storm is to directly hit my beach. The prospects are bad.

"We worked on. He dropped the plywood, and it came quickly down missing my head by inches and shearing off a tender green new stalk from my Bird of Paradise. "Sorry," he said. "Slipped." I thought of my wife and son who, four blocks away, were supposed to be getting sandbags. Just as I thought about them, they returned, reporting that there was a massive line with a fight breaking out over the sandbags. They showed me thirty pillowcases they bought at the thrift store, which they had filled with sand from a dirt lot. "Brilliant," I said. They began sandbagging the garage door, all the way across and two pillowcases high. "It's futile," I thought.

"The partially drunken man finished the windows without incident. The wind continued to pick up. "How much do I owe you?" I asked. "Nothing. In times like these, we got to help each other." He grabbed up his tools and left before the mandatory evacuation, which took effect less than two hours from his departure. We hurriedly filled our cars with scrapbooks, jewelry, paintings, a three-day supply of clothes, and some guns that had been my grandfather's."

Later that night, sixty miles inland at a Presbyterian Conference Center in Starke, Florida, I wrote:

"I don't know what to feel. To think. To pray. To hope for. I'm sixty miles from my home, which is being flooded or will be flooded. Destroyed or will be destroyed. The wind keeps pushing the palms tree in the backyard and the giant pine tree has probably been toppled. The oaks branches have surely been ripped from the bodies of their trunks. The tidal surge grows, and the storm will hit exactly at high tide. And I don't know what to think. To pray. To hope for. I don't want to feel sorry for myself. But I do. There are others taking refuge here. People who will have it just as bad or worse. I need to be strong even as I am vulnerable. I need to put my trust in God. So easy to write. So hard to do…so impossible at this moment."

Two days later we returned, the storm having veered off the forecast trajectory. It missed us by thirty miles. The maximum sustained winds were only eighty miles per hour and the surge was only 3-to-4 feet. Nevertheless, we returned to a devastated community. Hard to describe. Businesses ruined. Hundreds of homes were uninhabitable. Four homes in our neighborhood took on water. But our home suffered only minor damage.

I kept the plywood that we hung over the windows — it sits in my garage. And I will keep the memory that in my hour of greatest need, it was not so much my faith that got me through the ordeal, but the goodness and faith of those who surrounded me.

65: Energy

Wind can devastate. But, without wind there would be no glide — except on those rare occasions when the plates of the ocean floor shift and crack and create unimaginable swells and almost certain damage to cities, towns, and villages along the coast. Wind can be nurturing and soothing to the wave and rider of the wave or the wind can act like a drunken fool, tossing, heaving, and weaving, making the ride difficult, if not impossible.

In the Greek language of the New Testament, as well as the Hebrew language of the Old Testament (Hebrew Bible), the word wind also can mean breath or spirit. In the first book of the Bible, Genesis, we read in the opening lines,

1 "In the beginning when God created the heavens and the earth, 2 the earth was a formless void and darkness covered the face of the deep, while a wind from God swept over the face of the waters. 3 Then God said, "Let there be light"; and there was light. 4 And God saw that the light was good; and God separated the light from the darkness. 5 God called the light Day, and the darkness he called Night. And there was evening and there was morning, the first day."

It's rather easy to see how the word spirit and wind are interchangeable. We cannot see the wind, just as we cannot see the spirit.

We cannot see the energy beneath the waves — the spirit of the waves — but we now know that the spirit beneath the wave and in the wave is energy — mechanical energy, a living and moving force that pushes the water up as it moves ever forward and outward, father and farther from the source of its genesis. This mechanical energy of the sea is to be distinguished from the other type of energy found in the sea — thermal.

Surfing, by its very nature, is built upon this spirit-energy, infused with wind and sun.

66: Weekend Warriors

Surfers who understand that the glide is crucial to their lives—those who have made surfing a lifestyle—are always attuned to the wind even as they are attuned to the tides. But not all surfers understand the glide as crucial to the lives they live.

As with all pursuits, surfing has its weekend warriors and those who paddle out only when the conditions are supreme. I will never knock the weekend warrior, those people who either by necessity or choice only paddle out on Saturday or Sunday. And I won't knock the people who only paddle out when the waves are perfect.

There is the tendency in the surfing community, however, to belittle the surfers who do not regularly and or consistently surf. I look at it this way: If these surfers surfed all the time the water would be that much more crowded. Do I like extra souls in the lineup on the weekends or on the epic days? No. Certainly not. But fighting the battle of weekend warriors is an impossible battle to fight. It would be like fighting the rain, fighting a falling, or rising tide. Impossible. Fruitless. Vain. Instead, I try to practice gratitude that the weekend warrior does not surf Monday through Friday.

67: New Boards

Recently, I got a new surfboard, and even though the waves were flat, despite the wind blowing from the southeast near gale force, despite the late February water temperature being 63 degrees — despite all these factors, my joy at having a new board prevailed over the temptation to wait and paddle out when the waves or wind improved. Hope springs eternal.

I grabbed my board, set it in the side- saddle on my bike and pedaled to the beach. Not a person anywhere to be seen, except a few anglers on the pier. It was late afternoon, and the sun was only 30 minutes from setting. Dusk was in the air and painted on the sky with large brushstrokes of orange. I walked to the water's edge, a skip in my step, a lightness of being, new board under my arm as I weighed its balance and wondered how it would trim, turn, and float. I noticed the glint of the dying sun reflecting off the bottom of the purple board and I felt like a kid. A new board has the power to take a middle-aged man and give him the heart of a child at Christmas.

Maybe all sports and hobbies are like this. Maybe the bowler who gets a new ball is transformed into a kid as she carries her new ball to the alley. Maybe the golfer or tennis player feels each step lighten as they head to their respective arenas. And yet, I still believe there's something different about surfing, exactly because the arena we play in is alive with energy and creatures and silence. More than a mere tool to get the best job effectively done, a new board is an instrument to higher consciousness. It is a sacred thing and a muse to happiness. But happiness is not always easily found.

68: Depression

In 1835, a man visited a doctor in Florence, Italy. He was filled with anxiety and exhausted from lack of sleep. He couldn't eat, and he avoided his friends. The doctor examined him and found that he was in prime physical condition. Concluding that his patient needed to have a good time, the physician told him about a circus in town and its star performer, a clown named Grimaldi. Night after night he had the people rolling in the aisles. "You must go and see him," the doctor advised. "Grimaldi is the world's funniest clown. He'll make you laugh and cure your sadness." "No," replied the despairing man, "he can't help me. You see, I am Grimaldi!"

Many in America might say the same thing about themselves. "I am Grimaldi!" We are the wealthiest, most powerful nation to ever grace the face of the earth. We have it all, right? Bigger and bigger flat screens, low interest rates, cheap clothes, and new iPhones. So why do so many of us consult our doctors about depression? Depression claims about 9.6% of America's population. That's somewhere close to thirty million people. This number is higher than any nation in the world.

In 2000, Kalle Lasn and Bruce Grierson authored a short article for the Utne Reader entitled, "Why is America so Depressed?" They noted that America is hurting because we are:

• Always, always on the go, seldom if ever taking a quiet moment to reflect.

• Willing to plunge deeper and deeper into debt to finance shopping sprees for nonessentials.

• Unshakable in our conviction that happiness is as close as the next stock split, breast augmentation, or Mazatlan vacation."

More recently, it has been said that our high depression rate stems from an overabundance of choices. In the face of so many choices, we become lost, always trying to choose the next best thing that will bring us status and approval. But depression, of course, is not always tied to the reasons cited above. Often it is a chemical imbalance. Sometimes you simply have it in your blood. I am one of those who have depression. I am treated for it and am grateful for the art and science of medicine. As a rule, people don't choose depression. Depression is like a wet blanket thrown over the joy of life. It's like living in black and white. Life doesn't feel 3-D. Depression impacts relationships and engagement with daily demands. It's no fun. Thankfully, I've only had two bouts with depression. Thankfully, surfing acts as a medicine of sorts, though never replacing anti-depressants prescribed by my doctor. To glide on a wave is to engage the imagination and a hope that may be hard to muster on land.

To some people, depression may even suggest disease – and very few parishioners want their pastor to have dis-ease. Dis-ease or disease suggests weakness, either physical or mental. Or even spiritual. So, pastors who do have depression secret their condition away, stuffing it behind a ready smile and joyful presence, while groaning inwardly for authenticity.

I once opened up to a parishioner about my depression. I thought I would test the waters. I thought the parishioner was a "safe" person to confide in — to be real with. But the moment I mentioned the "D" word it was as if someone had slapped his face. His jaw tightened. His back stiffened. His body language screamed, "Get me out of here!" Noticing that he became uncomfortable with what I had just shared with him, I said something dismissive like, "Oh, I shouldn't have told you that. That is probably too much information." And to this, he replied, "Yes, probably so."

I understand that not everyone feels this way. Indeed, some parishioners have been helped by my admission of depression. But a great bulk of people have quietly stepped around the issue — as if they don't want to get too close to me for fear of catching the dis-ease.

Christian theologian and popular author, C.S. Lewis wrote in *The Problem of Pain*, "Mental pain is less dramatic than physical pain, but it is more common and harder to bear. The frequent attempt to conceal mental pain increases the burden: It is easier to say, "My tooth is aching" than to say, "My heart is broken."

So, is that what we have? Broken hearts? And why is this? Could it be that having it all and being it all is not a recipe for happiness but, in fact, it's nemesis? Life is paradoxical in that having it all doesn't equate to having more happiness. Even among those with chemical imbalances, depression is accentuated by chasing the tail of "success." Jesus was right when he said, "If you cling to your life, you will lose it, and if you let your life go, you will save it."

All said, I do like to get new surfboards. And while a new board isn't a cure-all or magic bullet that kills depression, a new board does act like a conduit and on-ramp to meaning, which is something that is often hard to find when one is depressed.

69: Hand-Shaped

A question arises from the consideration of a new board, and it is a question debated in the surfing community: All things being equal, is a hand-shaped board better than a machine-shaped board? Is there a difference in quality? Does a hand-shaped board trim better, turn easier, bring a more beautiful glide than a machine-shaped board? This question is on the minds of surfers —and especially shapers — because most boards that are sold in shops are machine-made. Some of these boards are made in the USA but many are made overseas. Truth be told, I have owned a lot of boards — both hand-shaped and pop-outs. And truth be told a second time, I have a tough time telling the difference, if, indeed, I can tell the difference. I have no doubt that someone like Joel Tudor or Kelly Slater can tell the difference. That said, I prefer a hand-shaped board by a local shaper. But to be fair, one of the best boards I've ever had was a machine-made board by legendary shaper Claude Codgen from Rockledge, Florida.

My new board, the one I referenced above, is a hand-shaped 9-foot,6-inch by Ken White. I watched him sculpt it. It's art. The board is a distressed purple color. Every time I get a new board shaped, I'm reminded of my very first custom board from Josh Autrey when I was primarily riding shortboards. It was in 1989 and I was 20 years old.

The feeling of getting a new board is complex — the emotions are mixed. On the one hand, the surfer is stoked to have the new board and cannot wait to ride it. On the other hand, the surfer is nervous that the board won't perform as well as intended, or, worse yet, the board will have no magic to it at all. Surfers pin remarkably high hopes on a new board: that it will be THE MAGIC BOARD — the board that is rare and elusive and just beyond the horizon of boards. It is a board that appears to read its owner's mind. The magic board is a thing that a surfer may hope to receive once or twice in a lifetime. That is why getting a new board offers such wide-ranging and complex feelings — because the feelings are built upon the diametrically opposed legs of hope and fear. Every new board offers the surfer unimaginable possibilities. To date, I have had only one magic board — a hand-shaped Natural Art out of Satellite Beach, Florida. Despite the rarity of the magic board, or exactly perhaps because of the rarity of the magic board, surfers live with great anticipation that each new board will be THE MAGIC BOARD. The hunt for the magic board is like the hunt for the lost city of Atlantis. It is a mythic quest —a spiritual quest.

The new board that I just picked up may or may not be magic. They jury is out until a decent swell. Hope remains alive. And yet, there is that small voice of foreboding that whispers doubt: "Your new board may not ride very well because the rails feel a little too full in the tail." The voice whispers this damnable possibility — but hope, the divine contrarian, counters these fears, whispering to me: "This could be the greatest board of your life."

As much as I need hope – and am a man of hope – I also know that history is the best predictor of the future. And what history has shown me is that a magic board is hard to come by. But the jury is out, and I remain hopeful, if skeptical of the new board.

70: Doubt

There are many little voices that whisper in our ears. There's the little voice of doubt and fear that speaks quietly, saying, "You are not smart enough, strong enough, good enough, handsome enough, rich enough, cool enough." The list is endless. There's the silent voice of fear or loathing that comes out when we are lying in bed at 3 a.m. searching for meaning or answers. This voice does its best to make us believe that life is set against us. But hope is alive. And hope, though sometimes harder to hear and more difficult to believe, stands as the eternal contradiction to fear. That's because hope is the language of God. While fear may be in opposition to the things of God (except for rational, natural fear of surfing a break like Teahpoo, Tahiti), doubt is not like fear.

Philosophy, art, and poetry have always welcomed doubters. Shakespeare, the bestselling poet of all time, wrote, "Modest doubt is called the beacon of the wise." Unlike philosophy, art, and poetry, however, religion is not always comfortable with doubt. In the Christian tradition, folks are often weary of doubt — and doubters.

One of the most notorious religious doubters in history was a disciple of Jesus named Thomas. In the Christian New Testament book of John, Thomas declares to his friends (who have recently seen the resurrected Jesus), "Unless I see ... I will not believe." One-week later Jesus appears to Thomas. In most English translations, Jesus says to him (dryly, I imagine), "Do not doubt but believe."

I want to clear Thomas' name. I want to clarify and redeem that odious title, "Doubting Thomas," which is an inaccurate translation of the original Greek text. In the original Greek, Jesus does not say, "Do not doubt, but believe." A more accurate translation is "Don't become unfaithful, but faithful." The difference between doubt and unfaithfulness is important, because one can have doubts, but still be faithful. Doubt, by definition, presumes some level of belief, for you cannot doubt that which you do not, at some level, believe. You must believe a part of something to doubt another part of the same thing. The issue for Jesus with Thomas, according to the original language of the text, is not that he might have doubts about the resurrection, but that he might lose his faith in the God of the resurrection.

Why get so nit-picky about a couple of words? The choice of words makes all the difference, and here's why: My experience suggests that religious faith is a two-sided coin. On one side is belief. On the other side is doubt. Living faith has aspects of doubt and belief. It's like Khalil Gibran, the third bestselling poet of all time declared, "Doubt is a pain too lonely to know that faith is his twin brother." Were it not for doubt, which is nothing more than curiosity or inquisitiveness, we would not grow in faith. Like a knife in need of sharpening, faith needs a whetstone to hone its edge—doubt is the whetstone of faith.

Doubt is a gift from God. It is not to be feared, but embraced, for God is greater than our doubts. Indeed, God uses our doubts to lead us deeper into the mystery of our faith. Doubt is like a door. And if you don't believe me, just ask Thomas.

Though doubt may be a healthy thing for spiritual faith, it is not always the most comfortable of emotions. It is especially not comfortable when the surfer picks up the new board and the voice of doubt begins its subterfuge of taunts. I can't say with any reasonable certainty how many boards I have owned over my 37 years of surfing, but I am certain that with each new board doubt spoke to me.

As a rule, I don't own more than three boards at a time. Longboards, unless you have ample garage space or an extra room inside the house, are not easily stored — because they are long. Their size makes owning more than a few difficulties for me. In reality, what would I do with a dozen boards? I can only surf one at a time and the surf conditions in Florida do not warrant many assorted styles of boards. From my experience, only two longboards are necessary in Florida: the everyday board that will catch knee-high surf and a board that can be used on days that are overhead, hollow, fast, or some combination thereof. If I had more space, I would have more boards, which may or may not be a spiritually healthy choice. I have found that the more I own, the more I am owned by the things I own. Most of the people I know, including myself, own too much of everything — from the size of our homes to the number of T-shirts, shoes, shorts, guns, books, jewelry, DVD's, and all manner of toys. On and on we go with the mania of owning things — as if owning stuff makes a life. Jesus was right when he said, "Where your treasure is there will your heart be also."

My treasure, in part, lies within surfing. The glide is liquid wealth. Today, I am a wealthy man. A large low formed off Cape Hatteras, North Carolina, and the buoys are reading twelve feet at 10 seconds. Closer inshore, the buoys are reading five feet at 10 seconds. At first light the tide was too full, too high for a good longboard wave. The shortboarders loved it. Overhead beach break. Tubes. Chaos next to the pier as every weekend warrior from Gainesville to Palatka descended upon the sea. I watched. I waited. I double-checked the wind forecast and the tides. Strategy is important. High tide was 7:05 a.m. The wind was 10 mph offshore. Knowing the break, and how the sandbar works with waves like this, I calculated that by 9 a.m., the waves would begin to break on the outside sandbar. By that time, the air temperature would be 75 degrees.

I returned to the beach at 9 a.m. with my new board that I decided to ride because then the waves were larger than chest high: a single-fin, with side-bites (extra fins) performance-style, 9-foot 2-inch board. The waves were just starting to feather on the outside bar. I paddled out. I did not recognize the other person, a young blond woman from the University of Florida. How did you know she was from UF? No wetsuit and the water was 65 degrees. Clearly a crazy. I surfed for three hours, and the waves were chest- to overhead-high. Strong, beautiful rights and lefts. Smooth drops, like being a kid and descending a tall slide on a playground. Solid walls. The waves pitched out, but not enough for barrels.

After the three hours of superb glides, I headed home, stripped off my wetsuit, climbed into my hot tub, turned the jets on and rested my shoulders, back, and deltoids against the pulsing water. I showered off, fixed a ham and cheese sandwich and some Minorcan clam chowder that I made the previous evening. I poured a glass of chocolate milk and then poured another. I ate my fill, curled up on our futon, blinds closed, a room full of shadow, and slept for an hour.

I woke to my wife and son coming home from my son's first soccer game of the season, which I hated to miss. But the waves were too good. We chatted for a while then my wife and I rode our bikes to the beach to look at the waves. And I was shocked. The waves were better. Much better. The form was as perfect as form can be. Due to the continual offshore wind, the waves were groomed to perfection. The surf forecast had suggested that the strong offshore winds and the diminishing low would kill the waves by mid-afternoon. But the forecast proved wrong. The tide was turning, just past low, heading high, and the waves were firing. And not one person out. Not one. I was stunned at my good fortune. I dashed home, two minutes by bike. Put the cold wetsuit back on, grabbed my board and was back to the beach in under 12 minutes. The waves looked like rifle barrels. Still, no one out. Strong offshores—but not so strong enough to create an east-flowing chop. The sun was high and warm.

The new board has full round rails, no discernable edge, except near the tail, a tucked-in nose, and a 5-inch rounded square tail. The board is 9'2" and set up as a thruster (three fins). The new board felt good under my arm as I walked to the water. Paddling out I could see that the board had more rocker than my other two boards. I tried to find the perfect center, the sweet spot for paddling, but it takes a while with each new board to understand its idiosyncrasies, virtues, and foibles, its personality and character traits, what it likes and doesn't like.

I paddled over a set of chest high peelers, the waves breaking exceedingly fast and hollow. And then I waited, my wife sitting on the beach next to the old concrete bulkhead that has some undiscernible spray paint in yellow and red. I waved to her, and she waved back. I waited. It was like the ocean decided to stop producing surf. Nothing. I felt like the sea had decided that it was not going to let me test ride the new board. It was as if all the energy in the Atlantic vanished into nothingness.

After fifteen minutes a set rolled in. I took the second wave and as I dropped in I got hung up near the top of the wave. The strong offshore wind was holding me back. I immediately wondered if it was the board, the wind, or some combination thereof. I took an extremely high line, and the board was like a bullet. The next several waves were similar, both rights and lefts. High, tight lines. Fast with good turns. Amy sat on the beach reading. She later told me that she happened to look up as I began paddling south, seeing a set on the horizon. She watched as I quickly spun, took off right, skating quickly across the top of the head high wave. As the wave hit a bowl-shaped portion of the sandbar, which is shallower than where I had taken off, the wave jumped up higher, spray coming off the back. I crouched low, my right hand dragging in the emerald wall, my wife watching from the beach as the wave pitched over my shoulders, the face curved and fine, full of grace and cylindrical precision. I flew down the line, pumping the big board, coaxing it go faster, pushing the newly christened Ken White Shape for all it was worth, pushing it to make the section, pushing it to stay ahead of the curl, pushing it to make the tube. Amy would later tell me that the wave was clear, cupped like a "C" and extremely fast. She would tell me how I disappeared behind the curtain and the scene was beautiful.

Though the new board felt a little uncertain under foot, my feet not dialed into the sweet spots, my knowledge of the board's personality still largely and mostly unknown, I felt pleased with the waves I rode and the glides that the ocean gave me. It was the fastest longboard I had ever ridden.

That night, after supper and the hot tub, I took the board down from the overhead rack in my garage, which houses boards, fishing poles, and the requisite American and Florida flags. It was dark in the garage and outside. I turned on the floodlights, the glow from the halogens illuminating the grass, ferns, pine straw, and iris planted throughout the beds alongside the split-leaf philodendron. I placed the board upside down in the grass. I muscled the fin partially out of the box and pushed and gently hammered it forward, tapping it like one might tap a knee to gage reflexes. The fin, a fiberglass 9-inch dolphin-style, was only six inches from the tail. The closer the fin to the tail the less the board will quickly turn. A single fin that is set extremely far back is for the classic nose-rider where a straight line is the most desired of riding positions. But for a board where maneuverability is more prized than nose-riding, the fin should be eight inches, or so, from the tail, depending on a person's style. Using my measuring tape, I tapped the fin until it was eight ¼ inches from the tail.

Fins come in distinctive designs and lengths for differing waves, boards, and riding conditions. I ride two different fin styles in two different lengths on three unique styles of boards. On my more performance-oriented board, I ride a thinner, more flexible fiberglass fin. On my nose-rider, I ride a fatter, stiffer fin. The fin for the nose-rider is thicker at the base than the performance-style fin. It also has less relief in the shape's overall curve. It is more full-bodied. However, I am not a particularly good nose-rider. I don't

186

have the cat-like grace required to cross-step with light-footed speed to the nose. Though I can cross-step all day long, and though I often may try for the nose (and occasionally get five off the tip, and even more irregularly get all ten off the nose), the board often sinks under my lack of elegance.

Like with most things in my life, I am not the best, but neither am I the worst. I am, however, dedicated. My life, as with my surfing, is not cut and dried, not black and white, but a mixture of grays. Surfing, like life, is complex and one size does not fit all. We are all unique and fragile creatures, and our surfing, as with our lives, reflects our tension between what and who we are and what and who we might become.

71: Change

To deny the reality of change, or to resist change to the point of some ideological nihilism, or because of a theological objection couched in holy writ, is an emotionally stunted intellectual position. We ought not defend a position or lifestyle, idea, or principle out of fear of change. If it is the fear of change for the sake of change, then our conviction is soft. Life is meant to be lived full throttle, without an abundance of fear, but with exuberance, passion, love, and the open embrace of change, for God is the very architect of change. And change is the heartbeat of hope. For just as with imagination, hope cannot exist without the reality of change. Without the possibility of change, hope dies. Even among those who say, "I hope nothing ever changes," the very wish that nothing changes is hope for change. For if one hopes that nothing changes this very hope suggests that change is needed for nothing to change. Change, as we all know, is the constant of the universe.

72: Travel

There is, quite possibly, no greater example of change than the ocean. The ocean is never static, even when it appears static.

Energy courses through the sea at a never-ending rate. The ocean is energy incarnate. As Jesus is God incarnate, so the energy created by God is incarnate in water. And this energy created by God is found everywhere in our seas, fueled by the sun's fusion, released into space in the primary form of light. The oceans are full of radiant energy and thermal energy based on the water temperature. All this energy results in a constantly changing sea.

There are five oceans in the world and seven ancient seas. I have only surfed in two of the oceans, the Atlantic and Pacific. I have snorkeled in the Red Sea off the coast of Egypt. I have snorkeled in Mexico, islands of the Caribbean, Kauai, Barbados, and the Keys. I have been to a total of thirty-six countries. I have traveled to forty-seven of the fifty states. While I am not a surfer who has surfed many exotic locations, or a waterman who has swum, dove, paddled, or sailed on many oceans or seas, I have been to a few places.

And while I may not be a world traveler extraordinaire, I have kicked up dust in more than a couple of international bars.

I have seen some spectacular ruins in places like Petra, Jordan, Mayan temples, Crusader castles in Syria, Scottish castles, the Alps of Switzerland, and France. I've floated on the Sea of Aqaba, cruised the coast of Turkey, and spent more than one night on the Aegean Sea. I'm no Jacques Cousteau or Cortez, but I've enjoyed fire-doused sunsets in distant lands like Lebanon, Greece, and Haiti. Travel, whether for surf or sights or both is the original education. Travel changes a person. My perspective has been changed from speaking with Palestinian children in the West Bank and the elderly in Hungary. Travel creates a horizon beyond the horizon.

Though my wife and I intentionally live below our means, and though we intentionally set aside money for travel, there always seems to be some "emergency" popping up: an unforeseen medical expense (basal carcinoma to cut out), new tires, new garage door motor, and new glasses. Broken dishwasher. New contacts. Car repairs. And then, of course, there is the necessity of saving for retirement and our only child's college education.

Expenses never end and so, saving for travel can be difficult. But not impossible. Week by week, putting a little aside here and there adds up. Like drops of water filling a bucket. Discipline, sacrifice, and sticking to a budget can make almost any travel plan a reality. For me, travel has become part of who I am.

73: Saved

As the early March wind blows hard and cool out of the southeast, I sit on the beach, my body buffered from the wind by the old cement bulkhead. I watch the ocean toss and heave, waves crashing, dumping on the inside sandbar, tossing and heaving and dumping on the outside sandbar. Whitecaps as far as I can see. No boats anywhere on the horizon. The wind is twenty knots —sustained — with stronger gusts. Black-headed gulls and two Royal Terns coast overhead, riding the wind currents, making fast and rapid adjustments in their flight patterns, their course reminding me of a drunken man weaving down an alley. As I watch the oceanic upheaval, I daydream of traveling to a locale with good waves, offshore breezes, and warm water. Though winter has been very mild, and though the water temperature did climb to 71 degrees last week, it has since plummeted back down to 63 degrees. Not too cold, but not tropical. And so, I watch the ocean and mind-surf, imagining that I am surfing excellent waves with the sun browning my skin and a cold beer waiting next to a pool, with coco palms swaying and soft reggae music playing in the background.

The chop on the ocean is supposed to fade in two days with an offshore wind to follow. I have planned the day, accordingly, moving a breakfast meeting and shuffling one other appointment to later in the day. The flexibility of my schedule is one major benefit to my vocation as pastor. Flexibility of schedule is a cornerstone to scoring the best waves. Flexibility is a cornerstone to the good life, as I define the good life. To be soft enough to bend, as the Tao Te Ching suggests, is key to living in harmony with others and oneself.

This harmony with God, others, and self gets at the notion of "saved" in the New Testament. Not long ago, I was walking in downtown St. Augustine just minding my own business, talking with friends, having fun, when suddenly a nicely dressed man came up to us and said: "May I ask you a question?" I wasn't sure what was coming next, but anytime in the Bible Belt that a guy in a dark tie and white short-sleeved Oxford shirt approaches you in public to ask you a question, you can be fairly sure that the question will be: "Have you been saved?" Once this question has been asked by the guy in the dark tie, my question becomes: "Do I engage the guy's question and talk theories of atonement, talk about Augustine, Luther, or John Calvin's soteriology, which would do little if any good?" Usually, I simply say, "I'm Presbyterian," which of course settles nothing for my interrogator. In fact, it usually prompts him to tell me that I am not saved. (Note: It's almost always a "him." There seems to be something deeply embedded in the male psyche that pushes men to try and convert people, which is really a synonym for conquering). The question remains, "Saved from what?" As far as I know, there are only two occasions in the New Testament that ever say what people are saved from, and it's not hell, it's not sin, and it's not the devil.

You cannot find, anywhere in the New Testament, a phrase that says, "Believe in Jesus and you will be saved from your sins or believe in the Lord

Jesus and you will be saved from hell." As strange as it may seem 99 percent of the time the word "saved" simply dangles in space waiting for someone to complete the sentence. The nicely dressed person who stops you and asks if you are saved may tell you the Bible says that if you believe a certain formula, you will be saved from hell. And though they may tell you this, it is always a good idea to ask them to show you where in the Bible it says exactly what they claim.

Maybe the question of being saved from something is left dangling for a reason. Maybe the New Testament, as a rule, never specifies what we are saved from because we need to be saved from so many things. I mean, we all need to be saved from something — something in our past, something that is currently casting a shadow over our lives, something that keeps us from being who God created us to be.

Maybe the question, "What are we saved from" is too hard. Maybe the question is too big. Maybe the question is, ultimately speaking, too complex for any one of us to answer. If this is the case – if questions of salvation are too big and complex for any one of us to answer – it is best if we simply trust that God can, and will, work everything out. Perhaps learning theological flexibility when it comes to matters of ultimate consequence is on par with learning to be flexible while surfing. If, when surfing, you are too rigid, it's unlikely that you will surf well. Rigidity and surfing, like life do not go well together.

74: Good Form

Wednesday morning rolls around and I am up when first light appears on the far eastern side of the Atlantic. Going into the bathroom, I notice that my left knee is aching from dancing the night before at the amphitheater with my wife. Last night, my wife and I went with two good friends, to see Willie Nelson. The dude's eighty-four and still jamming. I look out my bathroom window and see the fallen brown oak leaves shuffling from west to east. Offshore. The leaves tumble across the green grass and across the pine straw bed that is close to the house. The leaves blow gently, they do not race.

I walk to the back porch, take my full wetsuit from the hanger, and put it on, its rubber cold and damp. There are few feelings worse than putting on a cold, damp wetsuit. I go to the garage and pull a board off the rack and slide it into the bike saddle. In two minutes, I'm looking at the ocean, which is mostly glassy. The waves do not look great, but the sunrise is lovely. The sun is just up, a thin line of burning orange poking up from the sea. It's dull and unbrilliant, thick, and pretty. The wind is 10 to 15 knots out of the south-southwest. Spray is coming off the waves, which look small.

I hesitate and take a long, slow look and decide to wax my board and paddle out. I don't use a leash. There are a few short boarders groveling for waves on the inside sandbar. Their lot seems pitiful to me. So much work for so little grace. So much energy for so little glide. I am the only one sitting in the outside lineup. The waves on the outside are not as bad as they appeared from the beach. About stomach-to- chest high with good form. There is a truism in the moment: things are not always what they seem. The rights are peaky and holding up well. I take a couple of waves and discover there's not much power in the swell. Lack of energy. The waves are breaking top to bottom, but they do so without much resolve. I decide to stop taking the smaller sets and wait on the larger sets — if there are larger sets.

On the horizon, a stack of lines, like corduroy, slant from the southeast. They approach my position at a strong angle. I paddle farther out and over the first wave. The second wave doesn't look good, so I let it pass beneath me. Just as the second wave rolls below my board, there is a third wave, much larger than the first two or any I've yet seen. And I'm in the prefect spot. Funny how this works. Sometimes we find ourselves in the best position imaginable for whatever life is about to offer us — and other times we are in a poor position to do much with what we have been given.

As the wave approaches, I spin, take a breath, and let it out slowly, paddle five hard strokes and catch the wave. I angle hard for an unexpected late right drop. The takeoff is steep, and I must step hard on the tail of my longboard to keep the nose from burying into the water. I make the drop and look down the line where the wave makes an A-frame peak. Racing toward the peak, I duck as the lip throws out and over me. I crouch and bend, and the soft sound encases me. The sound is distant, full, and gentle, but all encompassing. I'm tucked perfectly beneath the lip as it feathers overhead. The lip is so thin, so fragile looking that it seems like liquid glass. Through the lip I note emerging blue sky, which reminds me of a glacier I once saw in Glacier National Park in Montana. The sky is hazy through the faint-green color of the falling lip. The moment is exquisite and vanishes as quickly as it came. I make it out of the small tube and cruise to the shoulder.

There is no better way to start the day than getting a barrel on an unexpected green peak as the sunrise throws off easy morning rays. Every surf session brings surprise. Like an unexpected barrel or an outstanding sunset, a baby manatee, leaping dolphin, a perfectly executed turn, a good laugh with a friend, or a time of intense silence. By its very nature, the ocean is a body of surprise.

75: Despair

Many years ago, one late summer day I was surfing a break called "Middles," which is two miles north of my home break FA. Back when people were allowed to drive in Anastasia Park, Middles saw a lot of action. I was surfing with a few guys — I can't recall who and I don't remember the waves. While waiting for a wave, the guy nearest me got knocked off his board by the wing of a giant manta ray, which is a different kind of creature than a stingray. Manta rays are of two species, the giant and the reef. Giant manta rays live in the subtropical and the tropical Atlantic. They can have a wingspan of as much as 15 to 18 feet.

Earlier while surfing, I remember how we watched the giant manta ray leap from the water a couple of hundred feet east of our position. It was easily ten feet across, with a graceful presence and beautiful color. Later, as we waited on a wave, without warning and with lightning-fast movement, the ray swam beneath us and its wing hit the guy near me, taking him off his board as if he had been yanked sideways by a 500-pound gorilla. Life, like surfing, is rife with surprises — events that leave us full of wonder and joy, terror or despair.

My last two years of college were full of despair. By my senior year, I had become a full- blown nihilist, if a college student can ever be a nihilist beyond fad. I thought I believed in nothing, which itself is a belief in something. I reveled in my despair while at the same time cursing it. My senior year of college was my first deep taste of depression, which was born from a lack of hope. My hope, which was in a naïve understanding of God, was crushed by the questions of philosophy. My faith shattered like a dropped bottle on the pavement. It can happen to anyone. You base your life, purpose, the whole meaning of the universe on something — anything or anyone — and when that thing lets you down or disappoints you, when that thing no longer lives up to the great volume of meaning you have invested in it, well, life can crack. Sometimes life cracks wide open and the jaws of death stare you in the face — but then you realize it is not death itself, only the death of meaning. But the death of meaning means the death of hope, and the death of hope is the mother of despair.

I have had small cracks in life, like when my parents divorced and when a girl I loved broke my heart. Darkness came and for a time I was inconsolable. And the glide did not fill those cracks or heal those wounds. It helped assuage my pain, but it did not remedy the injury. The adage, "Time heals all wounds" may be true, but I'm not sure about the universality of this truism. It may be true, but my limited experience with wounds — physical, psychological, and spiritual – suggests that some wounds are healed only by the sweet sleep of death. Sometimes, only death cures the pain.

Death is not talked much about in our youth-obsessed culture. Everyone is always trying to look and live some idyllic snapshot found on Facebook or Instagram. We like to keep thoughts of death at arm's length.

When death does strike, I often observe people quickly wanting to skirt the subject, as if not talking about the one reality that we all share will somehow minimize the possibility that we ourselves will die. Death does not scare me. In fact, truth be told, I look forward to my death. I do not look forward to the process of dying or the possibility of accompanying pain — but death feels to me like release. Acute, chronic pain does scare me. But death, no. There is life afterlife. A glide after the glide. The life of flesh and blood is not the end of the mind or the energy that makes the mind possible. Death does not have the final word at the end of our life sentence. Death is a semi-colon.

76: The Sun

Sitting on my board, staring at the horizon, with the sun three hours up, I pondered my past, and what is yet to be. The morning sun reflected on the water's surface looked like a yellowish, glittering liquid road. The refracted light began with a narrow brilliance directly in front of me, and the farther I looked to the sea, the wider the yellowish, glittering liquid road became. The road had a wide cone shape. The dimpled water cast the rays of the morning sun directly into my eyes.

The sun is an amazing creation, sitting at 0.9934 atmospheric units away from earth — ninety-two million miles —its light (photons) takes about eight$\frac{1}{2}$ minutes to reach the earth, at a speed of 186,282 miles per second. The sun's power with its photons creates the brilliant yellow beauty we see from earth and its energy is what, in part, gives us the waves we ride.

Sitting in the water, I think about the magnitude of the sun and its influence as I wait for a little wave. I marvel at the sheer mystery of the universe and the entirety of life that is dependent upon this star, the sun, millions of miles away. I scan the sky, north of the sun, and the clouds are delicate and detached swirls of cirrus ice hovering high in the atmosphere.

Looking more westerly, in the direction of my home three blocks away, strato-cumulus patches – white and rounded with darker linings– are rolling toward the sea.

It amazes me to consider that clouds are composed of water evaporating from the ocean, lakes, rivers, mud puddles, and ponds. Clouds are a curious phenomenon. If the water vapor that clouds are formed from is invisible as it evaporates, then how are clouds visible if they are but accumulations of the invisible water vapor? And why are clouds different shapes and colors? And what makes a particular cloud hold its shape longer than other clouds? The answer to these questions is simple, if difficult for someone like me to comprehend. Heat turns water into vapor, which coupled with light refraction and the colder temperatures in the upper atmosphere, dance together to produce the phenomenon we call clouds. Watching the clouds, I am awestruck at God the engineer, artist, and physicist.

I am filled with awe at the beauty as I wait for a wave and watch the sky. My attention turns from the clouds and sun to the people meandering on the beach. Old and young, skinny and fat, tall and short. People, a few dogs, and a thin, a homeless man standing in long underwear holding a guitar. The last of these sights is very strange, as I rarely see homeless people at the beach and I've seen one in lng underwear holding a guitar. Not so strange is the man with a metal detector. He wears khaki adventure pants with zippers, a khaki shirt and a khaki wide-brimmed floppy hat with a drawstring tucked under his chin. He wears khaki boots with his pants stuck in the top of the boots. I chuckle to myself. He looks ready for an African safari. Ready to hunt lions. But instead of a high-powered rifle swung over his shoulder, he has a robust metal detector with a bright red handle attached to his right forearm. He swings the gangly instrument back and forth near the high-tide line. In his left hand, he has a spade to make a little hole in the sand. He turns the sand over and over, running his detector back and forth. A crowd has begun to gather and suddenly people are talking to him. He has become an unlikely beach hero.

I stop watching the khaki dressed man as a sweet and tiny set rolls through. I take the first wave, draw a high line, and walk to the nose, take another step toward the nose and immediately the nose tanks, and I fall. I barely miss the board, which could have been a painful face plant. The board drifts away because I am leash-less. The second wave of the small set breaks before I can get to my board. The board heads directly toward me at a good clip and I try to grab it, but it is too fast and goes all the way to the beach, the fin getting hung up on the sand. I swim, get the board, and decide to call it a morning after only six waves.

On the way back to my bike, I stoop down and scoop up a small, white arc shell. For the last six years, I've been picking up a shell after every surf session. I take the shell home and put it in a ceramic bowl with other shells from other surf sessions from the same calendar year. The maroon-colored ceramic bowl sits on my nightstand, so I see it every morning and every evening and I'm reminded of how much I need surfing. The shells act a container of memories. They help me remember the glide.

The importance of remembrance cannot be overstated. The importance of remembrance to the life of faith is critical. Faith is based on a remembered event that dovetails personal experience and communal practice to memory. Memory is the cornerstone to the active, historical spiritual life.

Without memory, without faithful remembrance, there can be no religious tradition.

To remember is an act of faith. Without memory, there could not be a historical faith. And while biblical faith has its deepest roots in trust of God, we trust, in part, because others have trusted before us. And we trust, in part, because we remember — if unconsciously — that our faith-forbearers trusted. Faith is a three-legged stool: trust, action, and remembrance. But without remembrance, trust and action are reduced to activities based solely in the present tense.

Jesus himself understood that faith and memory hold hands. They are wed together. One of his very last acts before being executed by the Roman Empire was to eat supper with his disciples in an upstairs room. In this upper room, as he broke bread and poured wine, he told his disciples to "Do this in remembrance of me, for as often as you eat this bread and drink this cup you proclaim the Lord's death until he comes, again." Without remembrance, the particularity of life and much of its goodness would vanish beneath the dust of history. We love because we remember. We believe because we remember. We glide because we remember —we remember the feelings of the glide, the stoke. Take away our memory of the stoke and the glide becomes an exercise like any other exercise. Memory helps to make the glide the glide.

77: Play

Many of the feelings that the glide evokes come closest to the way children embrace life – playfully. The glide, while deeply spiritual, is also deeply playful. Sometimes, or even most of the time, it is the play involved in the glide that keeps me wanting more of it. It is a spiritual play, one that is often infused with wonder and awe, which are, strictly speaking, religious words.

Regardless, if one leg of the glide is spiritual, the other leg is play. We surf because it is fun. Surfing makes us feel good. It is, or can be, a completely frivolous activity. At its best, the glide is nothing but itself, which is a playful spirituality.

The most play happens, for me, when I'm surfing with my son, William, or my good friend Joe. Watching someone you care about get a good wave after you, yourself, have gotten a good wave, is a feeling that's that is hard to describe. I feel like a kid on a playground. William or Joe drop-in, their face intent or serene, their whole body-focused, if relaxed. I feel like a kid in the water and there is a lightness of being. There is joy – but not under every circumstance.

There can be fear, anxiety, and dread. More than once while surfing bigger waves (big for a native Florida boy), I have felt stalked by discomposure and trepidation. Times in Barbados, Costa Rica, Kauai. Times surfing hurricane waves in Florida. I can only imagine what must go through the minds of people who surf places like Jaws, Mavericks, and Teauhpoo. Fear and dread of a quite different variety.

But dread and trepidation do not have the final word in surfing. Play and joy trump anxiety and discomposure. With play and joy comes a certain lightness of being — in the best sense of this phrase. Like when I'm sitting on my board in the middle of summer and the air is 95 degrees, the water is 80 degrees, and the sky is creamy azure. The water is a noticeably light green around my dangling legs and as I look out to sea the water becomes a darker teal and then farther out the water is almost turquoise. Waves roll in — no matter the size — and then my body, deep brown from the sun, paddles with a languid ease, rises and glides and then I am filled with a lightness of being known only by angles and small children.

The joy of surfing even extends, during my more contemplative moments, to periods of flatness — times when there are no waves to ride. About ten years ago, I remember this one moment during the summer when the ocean looked like a lake for weeks. My son and I rode our bikes to the beach and after looking for sea glass, we jumped in the ocean. The water was warm and quiet, the sky a dusky smattering of washed-out orange and pink and cobalt. There was no breeze. The air was still and sticky.

After splashing each other, wrestling, and jostling, we floated. Lying on our backs, eyes open to an endless sky, I sank into the salty arms of mother ocean. She held me gently, fully, and peaceably. Though I had floated on my back countless times before that moment, something about that experience, resting on the surface of the sea with my son, gave me a ... stoke ... as if I were surfing. Relaxing into the float, tranquility encased me. I surrendered to the ocean and spoke gratitude to God. A holy moment. A blessing. All things I feel in the glide.

In an odd, mystical way, the glide infuses other moments with bliss. The glide can transcend the glide itself — and this is part of the mystical side of surfing. Surfing transcends surfing. The glide is an enterprise unto itself.

Leaving the ocean with my son, that day, after wrestling and floating, we walked back on the beach, our skin air-drying under the sun, salt trails left behind by the evaporated water. We picked up shells, throwing them back and forth. We slung seaweed (from the Saragossa Sea, a region in the North Atlantic that is bounded by four different currents, which oceanographers call a gyre) at each other. Drying as we played, smiles wide as we passed driftwood and sea gulls, our hearts connected and full of easy pleasure.

On days like these, I relearn the meaning of life, which is to live, as a philosophy professor once said to me. So simple. The meaning of life is to live.

As a middle-aged man with a compromised core, shoulder, and knee issues, that is why I have become so reflective about surfing. I sometimes wonder when I will ride my last wave. It's like a friend once said: "At some point you put your child down and never pick her or him back up." Will I know my last wave? Will it be in one year or ten, twenty years or two weeks?

It's a hard and very odd thing to consider, the riding of a last wave. And I wonder if I will know that it is my last wave? Asking the question about a last wave feels a bit like asking, "When will I take my last breath?" or "When is the last time I will go to sleep with my wife, cuddled under a blanket, her hair smelling like wind and honey?

Surfing is part of the fabric of my being. Even when I am not surfing, my mind will go to the ocean, to waves. Not a day goes by that I don't at least consider the glide, the wind, tides, and beach. The beach has been a thread throughout my entire life. I remember being a young child growing up in very South Florida — back when parts of South Florida were still like paradise — sitting on the beach with my mother. Sitting in a tidal pool. Hermit crabs scampering around, me trying to catch them. Mangroves and coco palms with coconuts hanging over head. I remember a large brown wooden boat. Ugly and listing on the sand. "Haitians or Cubans," my mother said. "Left their home to come here."

The sea has always been an avenue for escape — for Haitians seeking a better life, Syrians, Puritans, Cubans, people from all over Europe, Asia, and the islands of the South Pacific. The sea offers something to those who sit on its sandy beaches looking at the infinity beyond their dreams, the vast expanse of water that plays tricks on the eyes and imagination. I see people like this all the time — vacationers from Atlanta or New York, Nashville or Ontario, the list is as wide as the ocean. These vacationers stream to St. Augustine in RV's and minivans, convertibles, and on motorcycles. They are old folks with a bluish tint to their hair seeking solace from the snow, and young families during summer hoping for the week of their inland dreams. They come hoping to unwind, to put their toes in the sand, to decompress from a life that has become hard to bear. They sit in folding chairs, wearing sunscreen and hats, holding fishing poles or orange plastic shovels. The grownups recline with a drink in their hand staring to the horizon, lost in their thoughts about a better life, a different life, or just lost in gratitude for what life they have back home. Many people dream of the Jimmy Buffet life as they sip a beer or a fruity cocktail, their children cackling like roosters as they build a sandcastle that will wash away at high tide.

Mothers unfold themselves from their beach chairs to walk to the water's edge, their toes cooled by the ocean, they look up and down at the beach, back at their husbands. They notice a sailboat heading south with two full sails, the jib dense with wind, a moving spec of whiteness against the sky that stretches to eternity.

And many of those who come for a week find themselves wondering, "What if?"

78: The Glide is Sacred

Our fleshy bodies are 60 percent water, give or take based on age, size, and gender. Newborns are as much or more than 75 percent water. It's no wonder that most of us crave the ocean. We are sea creatures, water animals. We are fish without gills, mammals without fins or flippers. But our hearts know what brings us a measure of peace in this world of never-ending emails and the tyranny of social media. And this peace of the sea is exactly why the population of Florida's coast has doubled in the last thirty years.

The glide seeks some of us out, and when we are found we are unable to resist its grace. The glide seduces us and our dreams for the future. The glide guides us to a board — borrowing, renting, or buying. And we learn if we are meant to learn. The glide is sacred.

I have taught more people to surf than I can count. But fewer than 10 percent ever continue surfing with any long-term commitment. The glide wasn't meant for all people. And that is fine. No judgment. In this way, the glide is like other pursuits. Everyone has their thing. And the glide knows this from the moment you step on a board. The transcendent quality of surfing reads us like a book.

Those of us who hear the call to stay with surfing, year after year, after injuries and near-death experiences, after lost jobs and lost girlfriends, after hours upon hours dedicated to something that cannot be understood from the outside, we know. Those who stay with glide, in good waves and bad waves, in cold and heat and long flat spells, we know. We know the power and glory of the energy that pulses through the ocean like blood through a body. We know the glide and the glide knows us. And there is no escape, even as we grow old and feeble.

Then, bald or gray, shriveled limbs with baggy brown skin, we sit on the beach or pier or boardwalk, and we watch the younger generation surf upon our shoulders. We watch and we mind-surf. As they paddle and slide, we paddle and slide with them, if only in our minds. We imagine their reality, and because we know the feeling, we can sense what is happening in the lineup or on the wave. The stoke transfers from the one surfing to the one who can no longer surf but watches from the beach. The mystery of the glide overshadows the experience of the one watching so that, in some spiritual way, the old and decrepit surfer who can only watch is one with the one gliding upon the sea. Both faces, tanned by the sun, smile after a good ride. The holiness is immanent.

Some might say that I overstate the glide — or, worse yet, sentimentalize surfing. Some might say my conviction that surfing is a numinous enterprise is hogwash, as we say in the South. Some might say that I am delusional. Crazy as a loon. A religious nut. Some might say I am all these things. After all, surfing is just riding a piece of wood or foam on water.

A simple, no big-deal activity: mere sport. But you will never hear me call surfing a sport. If the glide is a sport, then the glide is not the glide but something else. If the glide is a sport, then it is no different than football, baseball, or basketball. No different than bowling. But it is different. And, we must remember this, even as the glossy magazines are bought up by conglomerate media machines and makers of surf apparel sell their wares for billions of dollars and the competitors of the World Cup Tour become glass dolls clothed in golden thread. We must remember and not forget that surfing started as the play of royalty — the Hawaiian kings and queens — and that the energy we ride is of God, made by God, and given by God. In its simplest form, the glide is nothing other than spiritual nurture once thought befitting only royalty.

To our detriment, we forget that we ride on the original dynamism of the Creator of the universe. We must not forget that the glide began as a holy thing, and holy things ought not be reduced to anything less. Surfing may mean different things to different people, but at its core it is holy play to us all, no matter how we understand these two words.

I would not go as far as to say that surfing is a religion to me. But I would say that surfing is religious, in the etymological meaning of the word. Religious — to re-connect to God, the Creator of earth and ocean.

Is life like surfing or is surfing like life? Sometimes questions are more important than answers and as I find myself riding small, glassy waves at high tide, I am connecting to God. The beauty of the natural world is a natural revelation. The waves lead me to believe that God is among the tides, grains of sand, the pulsing force that runs through the sea. God is in the glide and the glide is in God. God is in the wave and the one riding the wave.

79: Atheism

Atheism and/or secularism are the fastest-growing (anti)religious sentiments in the United States. Some prominent atheists, such as Richard Dawkins and Christopher Hitchens, have even garnered rock star-like status.

Atheism is nothing new. 2,400 years ago, even the famed Greek philosopher Socrates was accused and condemned as an atheist. (But he was framed!). And though the Church has done its best through the centuries to stamp out unbelief, it not only persists, but is rapidly spreading.

With freedom of religion comes freedom *from* religion. Freedom from religion may be a natural by-product of religious freedom. Freedom of religion allows us to fall anywhere along a spectrum of belief, which may include unbelief.

Many younger people who profess atheism do not realize that atheism itself requires a leap of faith, albeit into unbelief. To be an atheist you must have faith that no God or gods exist. It is true that religious people cannot prove that God exists. But it is also true that atheists cannot prove that God does not exist. Both philosophical commitments stand upon a precipice of faith.

I recently read a blog that highlighted a European middle-aged man who was raised in the Church, but now labels himself a nonbeliever. This man was asked why secularism and atheism have stormed European cathedrals and country parishes alike. His answer: "Disenchantment with the integrity of religions." That should give all religious people in the U.S.A., whether Christian, Jewish, Muslim, or Hindu pause for reflection. It should give us surfers pause.

While I pay little attention to philosophic objections from atheists or secularists, I often pay attention to heartfelt critiques by formerly religious people. Disenchantment with the integrity of religions, I believe, is a major factor in the growth of atheism and/or secularism in the U.S. For some people, freedom from religion begins to look a lot like freedom from hypocrisy, pretense, and spiritual duplicity.

According to the European man who was interviewed, this "disenchantment" with the integrity of religions boiled down to people not living out their faiths. In other words, religious people were not acting like people who make up the religions they professed to follow and hold true. I suppose there will always be people who find fault with religion. But it might be worth looking in the mirror and, if we have spiritual leanings, asking ourselves a question: Do my words or actions (or inactions) as a Christian, Jew, Muslim, Hindu (fill in the blank) discredit belief in God?

As surfers, people of the glide, we might also ask ourselves an additional question: Do my words or actions as a surfer discredit the glide?

80: Great Waves

Today is September 18, which is the anniversary of my surf accident during Hurricane Igor in 2010. The water temperature today is eighty-three and I know this because like every morning, I called the surf report. The waves this morning are thigh-high and glassy but I can't surf this morning because I have my fourth funeral in a month. Weeks, like seasons, come and go. The tide always changes. My ability to catch a wave first thing in the morning isn't always possible. However, if a good swell is forecast, then I will rearrange my week around the waves.

Two weeks ago, a hurricane was forecast to bring us potentially epic waves. It traveled from the far Atlantic and was never a threat to land — at least Florida. It stayed a course that kept it 1,000 miles away, near Bermuda. It maxed out at a Category 4 hurricane with winds near 140 miles per hour.

Every surf forecasting model showed the high probability that we would score good surf.

It's rare that we get genuinely great surf in St. Augustine. Once per year. Maybe. It's exceedingly rare for us to get anything resembling the kind of surf that we all travel to experience. But this hurricane looked very promising and so, two weeks out, I began dismantling my schedule and rebuilding it around the surf. I rescheduled certain meetings and begged out of other meetings, citing a personal issue that had come up. I cleared my calendar for Wednesday, Thursday, and Friday.

It's as if I was getting ready to meet the president. Or my savior. Everything else was put on hold. And that is the spiritual nature of surfing. It's like a calling. Like hearing a voice saying to put aside other pursuits or obligations to fulfill your purpose. While this may be too strongly put, I don't think it's too much to say that surfers who've been surfing for a great deal of time, through the ins and outs of life, who have made sacrifices to stay in the water, who in their later years incorporate activities to strengthen their bodies that are beginning to fail them — this is a calling. An avocation. A dream of the heart that gives them hope and meaning. And what is more important to human life than hope and meaning?

81: Vulnerable

I remember this one time when I was surfing just as the sun came up. The ocean was dense with fog. It was hard to see the waves. The pier was barely visible to my south. The water was silky glass. I found myself fretting that a larger wave would roll through, and I would get caught inside.

It is a strange thing to be in the ocean when visibility is extremely limited. I always feel vulnerable. When fog blankets the sea and I strain to see the waves that are marching like disciplined soldiers to the beach, I am keenly attuned to the slightest penetration of the sun.

On that day, this was the case. I felt vulnerable, which is an emotion that I was taught to stuff, keep down, not let out. Vulnerability, while important in the development of a deep inner world, was not something I was taught to value.

I was taught that a man ought to know how to shoot a gun and hook a fish. I was taught, as was every other good Southern boy, that a man opens doors for women and pulls out chairs for them. A man never hits a woman. I was taught that a man does not back down from a bully. A man is tough and does not cry. A man is generous and a defender of those weak in body or mind. A man does the best he can with any job given to him. A man always follows through on a promise. A man is a good provider and never cheats people. A man always carries cash and a pocketknife. These things comprise a man's character.

So went the *man-isms* of my father. So went the mantra of character through childhood and my teenage years as a white, Southern male growing up in the atmosphere of a country club. While I was comfortable in the world my father provided for me, I was not altogether comfortable with my father's worldview. After issuing one of his many man-isms, I would often feel less than the man my father willed me to be.

I spent my twenties thinking that my dad had it wrong, or at least partly wrong. Even as I wondered about my father's philosophy of a man's character and its insufficiency, I aspired to prove my manliness to my father. In my twenties, I lived like Zorba the Greek and Hemmingway — full throttle. I lived a dozen lives trying to prove to myself, and to my father, that I was a man, a real man. Ironically, he never noticed my conquests, or at least didn't acknowledge them.

Eventually, I accepted that my father's bar of manhood was not the true measure of a man's character. Manhood is more complex than any one description of masculine character.

For me, life began to change with seminary, marriage, and a child. Then, in my 40th year, my body got pulled apart while surfing Hurricane Igor. My mind trod the road of deep depression. Great humility crept in and took up residence in my heart. Vulnerability became a necessity in the daily tasks of life. I had to ask my wife: "Honey, will you please lift this slow cooker onto the counter for me?" I learned that I could not always be tough. Indeed, I could not even pull out the chair for my wife. Surfing was totally off the table. Sometimes the best a man can do is get out of bed and cry like a baby for what has been and may never again be. My understanding of manhood had to change. And, as it changed, character triumphed.

The manly character my father instilled in me is an old-school paradigm, one that I wish to not entirely discard but do wish to tweak. The narrative that I grew up with does not lack honor, virtue or respect. What it lacks is a certain depth, especially theological depth. And so, while I continue to embrace many of the man-isms my father instilled in me, and even as I pass them on to my son, my character now is not so much defined by my father's understanding of manliness, but by something my father considered the antithesis of manliness: vulnerability and gentleness. I have allowed my foibles and pain to be exposed — and to be OK with the exposure. Even more than OK, my wife has taught me to honor these foibles and pain and to use them to inspire greater depth in others as I let my armor down.

So, as I paddled out on that foggy morning feeling nervous and exposed to a larger wave that may roll me and beat me, I relaxed and tried to welcome the experience, the feeling of not being in control and acknowledging the reality of my situation. So much of life is like that: honestly acknowledging the reality of a situation or the pain of a person. That acknowledgment allows for greater fullness of being and authenticity. Realness. In a strange way, vulnerability can give rise to hope and meaning.

Combined, hope and meaning are like a third eye helping us see what cannot be seen. Surfers live their lives with this third eye turned to the horizon of aquatic possibility. Surfing gives us hope and meaning, even if the waves are short-lived, we have the hope that a new storm will generate meaningful waves. In a deeply existential sense, surfers find hope in storms. They find meaning in oceanic chaos, where the wind is fierce and churning up energy.

It's an odd thing to consider how surfers need storms, chaos, for meaning. Surfing can teach us to better appreciate the stormy times of life when chaos is the rule. It's in those stormy periods of life where meaning is found, and hope is renewed. Certainly, no newness comes from stasis. No grand tomorrow can come from inertia. In life, we must have periods that upset and upend existence if we are to mature, grow, and flourish.

This carries over to surfing. It's the times when I am pushed beyond my comfort zone that I grow. Like the time my wife, son, and I were Panama for two weeks.

We arrived at night when the buoys read six feet at 16 seconds. We couldn't see the surf but could only hear it. Within 10 minutes of s arriving, all electricity went out and I could barely make out my wife standing two feet away. Total darkness. except for the trillions of stars easily visible, and the Milky Way looking close enough to touch.

I'm not sure if it was the readings on the buoys or the fact that I couldn't see the waves — or because the electricity went out and made the place feel spooky, but I felt a touch of fear, a touch of vulnerability.

If we push through fear, control its hold on us, its former power can become our power and through it we learn to handle a larger dose of fear and uncertainty. Fear upends our existence, if only temporarily and mildly—but its presence signals we have moved beyond statis.

The next day, we checked the waves at sunrise. The surf was large. Not double overhead but well overhead and thick. "And you ride a longboard," I remember saying to myself. As we watched the sets roll through with little to no secondary or tertiary swells, I considered how I could make it out without incident if I paddled hard and timed everything exactly right. As we stretched, I imagined how I would make it to the lineup with the 9-foot orange and yellow board that was shaped for me for my fiftieth birthday. A single fin with a pintail and rounded point for a nose, the board has almost no rocker and is fast as the day is long. As I waxed it up, the coconut smell from the rounded bar of Sex Wax penetrated the air. Looking up with the bar of wax, I got a few strange looks from other people getting ready to paddle out. Their looks questioned my sanity. Watching other surfers watching me, I briefly questioned my ability to handle the surf, which broke over a sandbar and where there was no discernible uncomplicated way out. While I surfed much larger waves on a shortboard in my late teens, twenties, and thirties, like in Barbados, these waves would be the largest waves I had ever surfed on a longboard.

While I'm not the best surfer on the block, I'm certainly not the worst. I know and respect what I can and cannot do. I know my limits, and these waves would push them. And it wasn't the size as much as it was the shape. The waves weren't folding with soft and gentle ease. The more I watched the sets the more I felt scared.

My son and I hit the water at the same time, spread apart by twenty feet. The water was 80 degrees, and the sun was rising from just behind our hotel. We were still in the blue hour, as it's called in photography.

I stroked hard. feeling confident now that we were moving. The water was glassy and a light green and there was a slight offshore breeze. The fear was still with me when a set appeared on the horizon. It was a question of speed and timing: Could I make it to the outside before the first wave of the set broke? And if I didn't make it outside before the first wave broke, what then? Should I return to the safety zone of the middle trough and continue to the outside after the set pushed through?

For better or worse, I've never been big on retreat when the possibility for advancement is real. I paddled on, turning to see where my son was in relation to me and the set. The last thing I wanted was to get pounded with my longboard flying around and hitting him. With him far enough out of my way, I kept paddling. The set was bigger than I thought and moving faster than I would have guessed. I made it over the first wave with no major issue. Made it over the second wave with no issue. The third wave loomed larger than the other two, which is often the case. It started feathering as I neared the trough, and I was scared that I wasn't going to make it. Just as it began to fully break, I pushed through the back. Barely. I looked behind me to see that my son had taken all three waves on the head.

82: Awe

The ocean is a wild place. It's a dangerous place. It can hurt you, or the creatures that call it home can hurt you. So why do we go? Why did my son subject himself to the grueling experience of being pulled down, shaken like a rag doll? What is it about this wilderness, or any wilderness, that compels some of us to take our place in its arena?

I can't speak for every adventurer or waterman, but for me, being in the wilderness of the ocean, desert, or the woods can feel like ... possession. There's an abandonment that comes from being in the wild. There is something that comes over a person who believes himself or herself to be removed from everything civil and cultural — everything neat and tidy. This feeling is exotic. It makes one believe anything and everything is possible exactly because the usual restraints that confine a person are removed. Wilderness is the embodiment of liberty. But not all wilderness is "out there," beyond us or outside of us. There is also a wilderness within us.

I once spent a month in a Trappist monastery, which is a monastic order in the Roman Catholic Church. Ultimately, my love of recreation, wine, and women, so to speak, kept me from committing to the order. Plus, I am too much a Protestant. However, what I experienced in that month was a spiritual wilderness of sorts.

I have experienced wilderness in a lot of places: coming face-to-face with a grizzly bear in Glacier National Park, 12 days solo canoeing the New River from North Carolina to West Virginia, and 10 days solo canoeing the Suwannee River from the swamps of Georgia to the Gulf of Mexico, camping for a month on the Mexico -Texas borderlands watching banditos on horseback forge the Rio Grande River to raid campsites, climbing peaks in the Rockies over 14,000 feet, and surfing large waves at remote spots in Central America. But at the monastery, I came to see that the greatest wilderness is the wilderness of interior life.

Our English word "wilderness" is formed from the Old English, wildeoren, meaning wild and savage. I have been scared by bears, gorges, banditos, rattlesnakes, avalanches, large waves, and boiling rapids. But there is something equally terrifying about the wilderness within. It is a location where one encounters the devil of innumerable fears, insecurities, vanities, and the deafening growl of silence.

We are told in both Matthew's and Luke's Gospels, in the New Testament of the Bible, that Jesus sojourned in the wilderness, camping 40 days, and was tempted by the devil. After his 40-day solo trip, after engaging the devil within — or without — angels came to him. And this is where the wilderness within us is like the wilderness outside of us: they are both fiendish and beatific. The wilds of life, physically and spiritually, remind us that we live amidst powers greater than ourselves, and these powers have the muscle to change us.

The spirituality of surfing is born from this context, which is the wild. I have surfed in a wave pool, and despite the perfection of the wave, I did not experience the underlying transcendence of surfing. That leads me to believe that surfing out of its natural context is not surfing, which was born in the wild of the ocean. Without the dangers and uncertainties of the sea, surfing is not surfing. At least not in its natural, spiritual form. That's not to say that riding waves in a wave pool isn't fun, it's just to say that riding waves that are generated by a machine lacks the substance of the mystical. Nothing is left to chance. Everything about the wave in a wave pool is known.

Additionally, there is the unnatural noise and composition of the experience, which takes place in a concrete lagoon. Surfing is a wild activity and needs the wilderness to be what it is.

Part of the wildness that gives surfing its edge is the spirituality that infuses each glide. Spirituality, as I have said, is the recognition of the force or energy that undergirds all of life. It is the life beyond life created by God. This primordial energy, which is the substance of all things, is wild beyond control or manipulation. It is this wild thing that surfers ride upon — the waves of energy in the form of water. Surfers engage in an activity that is, at its core, a practice of appreciating this wild force and energy.

Even among hardcore atheist surfers there is a respect for the otherness of the glide. There is a recognition that surfing has a depth that golf or baseball does not have. This depth may not be called spiritual, but it is something beyond the ordinary. And when something is beyond the ordinary it is either extraordinary or transcendental — or both. Either way, the depth of the glide is owed to the energy that makes it possible. And this energy, whether labeled religious or not, is wild —beyond control. For those of us who believe in a higher power, of whatever form, this energy is created by God. The pure act of surfing is a connection to our higher power by virtue of the energy we ride upon.

Once, my son and I rose before dawn and biked to the beach to surf waves from a hurricane. The enormous energy generated by this storm took the better part of a week to make it to St. Augustine Beach. It took time for the waves to be born, to grow, to mature, to coalesce into something beautiful. The waves were 5 to 7 feet, and the wind was offshore. The sunrise was burnt orange with streaks of lavender.

The spirituality of the moment was accentuated to a degree that brought me significant awe. Awe is the place of transcendence, when you know that you are part of something much larger and greater than yourself. Awe is the place of resurrected idealism, where we feel that all things are held together by God and will find their place in God — the waves and surfer among them.

Made in the USA
Las Vegas, NV
19 June 2022